PERSPECTIVES

ON YOUR CHILD'S EDUCATION

BOOKS IN THIS SERIES

Leonard G. Goss, Series Editor

PERSPECTIVES

ON YOUR CHILD'S EDUCATION

4 VIEWS

MARK ECKEL

G. TYLER FISCHER · TROY TEMPLE

MICHAEL S. WILDER

EDITED BY TIMOTHY PAUL JONES

B&H
ACADEMIC

NASHVILLE, TENNESSEE

Perspectives on Your Child's Education

Copyright © 2009

All rights reserved.

ISBN: 978-0-8054-4844-3

Published by B&H Publishing Group
Nashville, Tennessee

Dewey Decimal Classification: 259.1
Subject Heading: MINISTRY \ CHURCH WORK WITH FAMILIES

Printed in the United States of America

1 2 3 4 5 6 7 8 9 10 11 12 • 17 16 15 14 13 12 11 10 09

VP

Dedicated to our children

Hannah Jones

Madeleine and Kathryn Temple

Madelyn, Layne, Karis, and Elyse Fischer

Tyler and Chelsea Eckel

Daly, Ashton, and McKenzie Wilder

Contents

Contributors

Mark Eckel is an educational consultant, director of the Mahseh Center (www.mahseh.org), and an academic member of the Heartland Fellows (www.heartlandfellows.com). For twenty-five years Mark has served the Christian education community as a high school teacher, professor, and speaker. Christian schools throughout the world use Mark's book *The Whole Truth: Classroom Strategies for Biblical Integration*, as well as his curricula Let God Be God and Timeless Truth. Mark earned the master of theology in Old Testament and is a candidate for the doctor of philosophy degree. Mark's wife Robin is a Christian school teacher; their children Tyler and Chelsea have been educated in Christian schools.

G. Tyler Fischer has served as headmaster of Veritas Academy in Lancaster County, Pennsylvania, for twelve years. He is also a board member for the Association of Classical and Christian Schools (ACCS). He serves as managing editor of the Veritas Press Omnibus curriculum—a course of study for secondary school students that guides them through the great books of Western civilization. He is a graduate of Grove City College, where he received a bachelor of arts degree in history, and of Reformed Theological Seminary, where he earned the master of divinity degree. He lives in Lancaster County, Pennsylvania, with his omni-competent wife Emily and four rather darling daughters—Maddy, Layne, Karis, and Elyse.

Timothy Paul Jones has authored, coauthored, or edited more than a dozen books, including *Conspiracies and the Cross, Misquoting Truth, Christian History Made Easy*, and the CBA bestseller *The Da Vinci Codebreaker*. After fourteen years in pastoral ministry, Timothy now serves as associate professor of leadership and church ministry at The Southern Baptist Theological Seminary in Louisville, Kentucky. In addition to a bachelor of arts degree in biblical studies and the master of divinity degree, Timothy earned the doctor of philosophy degree from Southern Seminary. His research has earned the Scholastic Recognition Award from the North American Professors of Christian Education, as well as the Baker Book House Award for theological studies. Timothy, his wife Rayann, and their daughter Hannah reside in the city of St. Matthews, near Louisville, Kentucky.

Troy Temple is lead pastor at the Indiana campus of Highview Baptist Church and associate director of the International Center for Youth Ministry. He has earned the bachelor of science and master of arts degrees from Liberty University as well as a doctorate in education from The Southern Baptist Theological Seminary. Troy has served churches in Florida, Virginia, North Carolina, Kentucky, and Indiana. He is actively involved in developing youth ministry programs at seminaries in Mexico and Ukraine, where he has served as a guest professor. He taught youth ministry at Liberty University and now teaches in the youth and family ministry programs at Southern Seminary. Troy and his wife Karla live in Jeffersonville, Indiana, with their daughters Maddie and Katy.

Michael S. Wilder has served the church as a pastor and youth pastor for more than fifteen years and is currently involved in a church plant in southern Indiana. He also serves as assistant professor and associate dean of doctoral studies in the School of Leadership and Church Ministry at The Southern Baptist Theological Seminary. In addition to a bachelor of business administration degree from Clayton State College and a master of divinity degree from New Orleans Baptist Theological Seminary, Michael earned the doctor of philosophy degree from Southern Seminary. He has co-authored a book on the transformative effects of short-term missions (B&H, 2009). Michael and his wife Ginger reside in Jeffersonville, Indiana, with their three daughters, Daly, Ashton, and McKenzie.

Acknowledgments

This book began at K.T.'s Restaurant in Louisville, at a table with Michael Anthony, Gary Bredfeldt, Dennis Williams, Kenneth Gangel, and Kenneth's wife Elizabeth. After noting that he was taking off a few months from writing books, Michael Anthony commented that someone ought to edit a perspectives or multi-views book on schooling options for children. Kenn Gangel said he thought such a book was published at some point in the past, in the 1980s as he recalled.

My tablemates agreed that a book of this sort was needed. I wondered aloud if anyone at the table was presently planning to come up with this sort of text. Everyone shook their heads, with Kenn Gangel declaring he had only one more book left in him to write. To this Elizabeth replied, "The first time he said that was three books ago."

I asked, "Would anyone have a problem with me pursuing a perspectives book on schooling options?" Heads bobbed in affirmation, and I immediately began mapping out this book. Within a few months, the process of putting it together was well underway. And thus the book began, over grilled salmon and Caesar salad at K.T.'s Restaurant. The text came to its completion at Starbucks on Shelbyville Road in Louisville, fueled by far more shots of espresso than any reasonable person ought to imbibe.

Thanks are due to so many people who have been responsible, at some level, for bringing this book from ephemeral concept to the volume you now hold in your hands. Mike Nappa of Nappaland Literary Agency masterfully guided me once again through processes of proposals and contracts. Terry Wilder and Jim Baird offered helpful assistance as the book developed. Without such superb chapters and responses from Mark Eckel, Ty Fischer, Troy Temple, and

Michael Wilder, this book would not have been possible at all. Thanks to each of you for your work.

Randy Stinson, dean of the School of Leadership and Church Ministry at The Southern Baptist Theological Seminary, continues to do an outstanding job of encouraging his faculty to pursue writing projects such as this one. By grading immense mounds of book reviews and student worksheets while this book underwent many drafts and edits, my Garrett Fellow Lilly Park carved out the extra time that I needed to complete this project. Steve Yates assisted Michael Wilder in his research; Chris Flora read an initial draft of the book and offered many helpful comments. When I lost half the content of the book in a freak computer network accident, Brenna Whitley and Kimberly Davidson helped me to put the pieces back together.

Thank you to my wife Rayann and my daughter Hannah, who endured many late evenings with me during the week of the infamous "Day that Daddy Accidentally Deleted His Book." I love both of you more than I could ever capture in the frail words poured upon these pages. And a special thank you to Hannah for the celebratory gift, upon my completion of this volume, of a box of double chocolate biscotti—which I think I shall go eat right now.

Preface

It is a choice that every parent must make—and, for Christian parents, it can be a difficult decision: "Where should I send my child to school?" This book brings together several theorists and practitioners to provide the information you as a parent need to make this choice. Our goal is to help you to discover which schooling option God will use to glorify Himself in your family.

Perhaps you have picked up this book because summer break is quickly fading and you must make a decision on schooling options quickly. Or maybe your choice is already made, and you are trying to figure out why anyone would make any other choice. Perhaps you have made a decision in the past, and now you wonder what you might have missed. Whatever your motivations, this book will provide you with the information you need to make a well-informed choice about your child's education. Additionally, if you happen to be a homeschooling parent, a Christian school teacher or administrator, or a Christian teacher in a public school, this book will equip you to make the greatest possible impact in your particular context.

Perspectives on Your Child's Education

In this book, proponents of four very different schooling options present their positions on how parents should answer the question, "Where should I send my child to school?" When it comes to each position, every contributor is both a theorist and a personal practitioner. Troy Temple, lead pastor at the Indiana campus of a multi-campus mega-church and the associate director of the International Center for Youth Ministry, is convinced that every Christian parent should consider public schooling. G. Tyler Fischer, headmaster of Veritas Academy in Pennsylvania, disagrees with Troy's position. According to Ty, no one— Christian or non-Christian—ought to consider public education. Ty believes the best educational option for everyone is an open-admission Christian school, a Christian academy open to enrolling students from both Christian and non-Christian families.

Mark Eckel, director of the Mahseh Center and a Christian school consultant, agrees with Tyler that Christian education is the best option. Yet Mark disagrees when it comes to who ought to be enrolled in a Christian school. According to Mark, the most effective schools are covenantal Christian schools—academies that enroll students from believing homes and partner with Christian parents to train these students in a distinctly biblical worldview. Michael Wilder, associate dean for doctoral studies at The Southern Baptist Theological Seminary, takes a fourth perspective. He believes that the finest schools may not be found in school buildings at all. Michael's family practices homeschooling, and he contends that the best context for your child's education could be inside your own home.

The content of this book particularly interests me because I have personally experienced all four options—two years in public school, three years in covenantal Christian schools, three years in an open-admission Christian school, and four years in homeschool. When my wife and I adopted our daughter Hannah, we first enrolled her in an open-admission Christian school that employed Maria Montessori's teaching methodologies. A year or so later, we recognized that Hannah needed far more one-on-one instruction than the Montessori school could provide. This week, we have just launched our fifth year of homeschooling Hannah, but we were looking at other options for our family. As such, wrestling with these decisions is not a mere academic exercise for us. It is a real-life struggle to discern what sort of schooling will best help our daughter glorify God with her life. As I face these options, I find it enlightening—and a bit comforting—to know that our spiritual forebears faced some of the same struggles that we face today. Look with me briefly at how some past Christians dealt with these decisions.

When Schools Were Pagan

Once upon a time, the schools that were available to most people were not merely secular. They were utterly pagan. Local officials and parents expected schoolteachers to reverence all sorts of false gods. Yet, as a teacher, any mention of Jesus Christ as God could result in public ridicule, even dismissal from employment.

Faced with such a system, one popular Christian writer argued that all Christians should pull their children out of the schools. "We renounce your wisdom," he declared to any schoolteacher who was willing to listen, "and we no longer concern ourselves with your tenets. We follow God's Word instead!"[1] And many parents did pull their children out of these secular schools. Such parents apparently provided the rudiments of their children's education at home, using biblical texts instead of pagan literature.[2] Perhaps these parents were inspired in part by ancient Jewish educational practices; even when Jewish families sent their sons to synagogue schools, they still viewed their home as the primary place of education and the father as the primary teacher.[3]

Not everyone agreed with this tactic, though. One opposing pastor admitted that most schoolteachers were "allied with all sorts of idolatry,"[4] yet he recognized that Christian children still need quality schooling. After all, even though their education might be filled with falsehoods, children need some "means of training for all areas of life."[5] And so, while refusing to allow Christians to serve as schoolteachers, this pastor urged Christian

---

1. Tatian, *Oratio ad Graecos, Appendix: Tatiani Fragmenta,* ch 1, ch 26: http://books .google.com/books/pdf/Oratio_ad_Graecos.pdf?id=057kZUS5h14C&output=pdf&sig=AC fU3U2w-4YjJ_d9S1SUwFbtiOoAfjO2Zg.

2. O. M. Bakke, *When Children Became People,* trans. B. McNeil (Philadelphia, Penn.: Fortress, 2005), 204.

3. Ibid., 176.

4. Tertullian, *De Idolatria,* 10: http://www.tertullian.org.

5. Ibid.

parents to enroll their children as students in the secular schools: "How can we reject secular studies," he asked, "when these studies are necessary to pursue divine studies? . . . [Secular studies] shouldn't be allowed, but they can't really be avoided either."[6]

Around this time, a newly-converted schoolteacher had another idea altogether: Why not establish a Christian academy that, instead of disregarding pagan knowledge, provided a biblical perspective on every aspect of life and learning—even on pagan learning?[7] Within a few decades, the church-based Christian school where this teacher served as headmaster became known as one of the finest educational institutions in the world. Even non-believers enrolled in the school to learn literature, science, rhetoric, physics, geometry, astronomy, logic, and history. Despite periodic persecution, these sorts of schools also spread to other cities. In some cases, these schools seem to have enrolled only Christians; much of the time, however, the student bodies of these academies included believers and non-believers.[8]

When and where did all of this happen?

No, it was not in twentieth-century North America.

Not even in England or the European mainland.

These events occurred in the Roman Empire, only a few generations after Jesus and His disciples walked the dusty paths of Palestine. As Christian faith spread beyond its roots in Galilee and Judea, Christian parents of the second and third centuries faced the crucial question of where their children would attend school.

Yet there was a problem: The schools that were most accessible to these parents were thoroughly pagan. The "encyclical studies" that formed the core of their education focused on the pagan poet Homer, with Hesiod, Cicero, and Virgil supplementing the Homerian epics.[9] The tales of the gods in some of these

---

6. Ibid.; cf. C. Dixon, "Who Nurtured the Child?" Paper presented at International Conference on Children's Spirituality (2000), 6.

7. Eusebius of Caesarea, *Ecclesiastical History*, ed. Kirsopp Lake, Loeb Classical Library (Cambridge, Mass.: Harvard University Press, 1980), 1:5:10.

8. M. Anthony and W. Benson, *Exploring the History and Philosophy of Christian Education* (Grand Rapids, Mich.: Kregel, 2003), 110–11; cf. E. Cairns, *Christianity through the Centuries*, 3rd ed. (Grand Rapids, Mich.: Zondervan, 1996), 104.

9. T. Morgan, *Literate Education in the Hellenistic and Roman Worlds* (Cambridge, UK: Cambridge University Press, 1998), 313–19.

texts were so immoral that even Romans wondered whether they ought to tell the stories to children.[10] But the problem was not just with the curriculum, as pagan feasts determined the sequence of the school calendar, and students learned their lessons in rooms decorated to honor pagan deities.[11]

No wonder, then, that Tatian the Syrian called for complete withdrawal from all secular learning in the second half of the second century: It was he who hurled the words, "We renounce your wisdom" into the faces of secular schoolteachers. Paganism was being pressed into children from every side, and Tatian feared for the future of Christian faith.

Tertullian of Carthage despised secular philosophies as much as Tatian: He wrote, "Away with every attempt to produce mixed-breed Christianity, composed of Stoicism, Platonism, and dialectics!"[12] Yet Tertullian knew that for Christians to proclaim the truth effectively among the pagans, Christian children needed training in rhetoric, logic, and literature. That's why Tertullian, writing a few years after Tatian, contended that, even though Christians should not teach in secular schools, Christian children ought to attend secular schools.

In the closing years of the second century, a former Stoic philosopher named Pantaenus became the first recorded instructor in the Catechetical School of Alexandria. It was here that Christian youth learned not only Scripture and theology, but also Greek literature and liberal arts. In the school at Alexandria, the wisdom of pagan literature was treated as a signpost, pointing to the divine wisdom that God had revealed in Jesus Christ. In the

10. Lucian, *Menippus*, 3–4: http://www.sacred-texts.com/cla/luc/wl1/wl176.htm: "When I was a boy, and listened to Homer's and Hesiod's tales of war and civil strife—and they do not confine themselves to the epic heroes, but include the gods in their descriptions, adulterous gods, rapacious gods, violent, litigious, usurping, incestuous gods—well, I found it all quite proper, and indeed was intensely interested in it. But as I came to man's estate, I observed that the laws flatly contradicted the poets, forbidding adultery, sedition, and rapacity. So I was in a very hazy state of mind, and could not tell what to make of it. The gods would surely never have been guilty of such behavior if they had not considered it good; and yet law-givers would never have recommended avoiding it, if avoidance had not seemed desirable."

11. J. Townsend, "Ancient Education in the Time of the Early Roman Empire," in *The Catacombs and the Colosseum,* ed. S. Benko and J. O'Rourke (Valley Forge, Penn.: Judson, 1971), 149.

12. Tertullian, *De praescriptione haereticorum*, 7: http://www.tertullian.org.

early third century, Clement of Alexandria succeeded Pantaenus as headmaster of the Alexandrian school. According to Clement, just as the Old Testament laws had prepared the Jewish people to receive Jesus Christ, pagan philosophies had prepared Gentiles for faith in Jesus. From Clement's perspective, pagan philosophy was no longer necessary after the coming of Jesus—but it could still be useful.[13] And thus the school in Alexandria became a highly-regarded one throughout the ancient world, even among non-Christians. In the space of a century or two, similar schools could be found in Jerusalem, Antioch, Edessa, Nisibis, and Constantinople. In some instances, these academies enrolled both believers and unbelievers. *v interesting*

Who Is Responsible for Your Child's Education?

I do not pretend that the issues or the solutions today are precisely analogous to the ones in the second and third centuries. Yet it is helpful to know that ours is neither the first nor the only generation to struggle with these issues. One crucial fact is clear from the writings of the early Christians: Parents were viewed as the persons ultimately responsible for their children's education. In contemporary culture, we have grown accustomed to releasing responsibilities for our offspring to professionals, handing off children's education to schools and their Christian formation to churches.

To be sure, when it comes to education, churches should equip parents, support families, and perhaps even work with parents to develop alternative possibilities for their children's education. Yet it is parents—not the church or the state—who bear the responsibility before God for their children's educational context. Regardless of where or how your child receives his or her education, you as a parent are accountable to participate actively in the curricular choices and in the educational processes. With that in mind, let's look together at four perspectives on your child's education.

---

13. Clement of Alexandria, *Stromateis,* 1:5–6: http://www.newadvent.org/fathers/02101.htm.

CHAPTER 1

Public on Purpose
WHY CHRISTIAN PARENTS SHOULD STILL CONSIDER PUBLIC SCHOOLING

By Troy Temple with Karla Temple

I grew up in a Christian home, and I spent eleven years as a Christian school student. I will always appreciate the sacrifices that my parents made to send me and my three siblings to Christian school. That school provided me with a foundational understanding of Scripture and doctrine that has sustained me throughout my life. Perhaps that was one of the reasons why, when the schooling decision faced me in my own household, it was one of the hardest decisions that I have ever had to make as a father.

At the time, my wife and I did not have the financial resources to send our children to any private school, Christian or otherwise. Both of us placed a high value on being a single-income family so that my wife could stay home with the girls. Although it was not an option I even wanted to consider, public school seemed like our only choice. For my wife, this choice was not nearly as difficult. She attended public school until she went to college, and her experiences were primarily positive.

Not so for me.

During two stints as a student in a public school, my exposure to such education had not been consistently positive. I attended public school in kindergarten. To that school's credit,

I didn't struggle academically when I shifted to Christian school in the first grade. My second taste of public schooling occurred during my junior year of high school. This was a far less positive experience, especially from the perspective of morals and ethics. As a result of that year's experience, I had difficulty even considering the thought of enrolling my child in a public school.

Here is what I eventually concluded, though: God had called us to train our children in the way they should go (Prov 22:6). In our family's particular circumstances, training our children "in the way [they] should go" would entail sending them to public school. In this chapter, I want to help you understand why.

What I Am Not Saying about Public Schooling

Before I make the case for Christian consideration of public schooling, I want to make it clear what I am *not* claiming. First, I am *not* proclaiming that all Christian parents everywhere should send their children to public schools. What I *am* suggesting is that Christian parents should not eliminate public schooling from their list of options until they have honestly examined whether God may be calling them to be involved in public school. Placing children in public school requires a personal passion that God Himself places in a Christian parent's heart. Unless you are certain that God has specifically called your family to embrace public schooling, *do not do it.*

Second, I am also *not* suggesting that public schooling is a possibility for Christians in every place. In some schools, especially in metropolitan areas, the schools are so large and the secular influences are so pervasive that a Christian parent's presence and protests will have little effect. Yet, as R. Albert Mohler has pointed out, the effects of the secular revolution in education are "less evident in more rural areas, with local political control more concentrated in the hands of parents."[1] Our family lives in an area where parents have retained greater influence in the public school system. Here, in keeping with Mohler's observations, "teachers, administrators, and students share an outlook that is at least friendly and respectful toward Christianity and

1. R. A. Mohler, *Culture Shift* (Colorado Springs, Colo.: Multnomah, 2008), 70–71.

conservative moral values.[2] Your community may not have a public school of this sort. If that's the case, *do not consider public schooling*.

Third, I am *not* suggesting that the choice to place your children in a public school must be permanent. In this present season of our lives, my wife and I are able to partner with our local public school in ways that strengthen our children and bring glory to God. I rejoice in the ways that God is using our witness right now. Still, I know that the day may come when God calls us to remove our children from public school. It is always possible that the culture of this school could shift. Such a shift could be so radical that my children's faith begins to be torn down. If that occurs, we will pursue other educational options for our children. So should you.

Whose Image Were My Children Created to Bear?

Some have suggested that all Christians everywhere should withdraw completely from public schools. This is the mentality I am seeking to avoid. Such sweeping claims could contradict the divine design for some families. God's intent for human families was to fill the planet (Gen 1:28) in such a way that God's glorious character and image would be reflected throughout the world (Isa 43:7; 1 Cor 15:49). If that is the case, the divine destiny of my two daughters is not to replicate my image everywhere they go. It is, instead, to fill the earth with the glorious image of God.

That means if my girls go to college somewhere far from me, they will be responsible to reflect a divine image in the dorm room. It also means that, as my daughters attend their public school, God's glory can be revealed through them. The same God who said, "Let there be light," is able to shine His light through them even in the darkest places, including a public school (see 2 Cor 4:1–6). Our family chooses to invest our energies in public schooling because of a calling to reflect God's image in that sphere.

As you choose your child's educational environment, I challenge you to recognize your choice as a means to a specific end.

2. Ibid., 70.

This "end" is *not* success in life but the reflection of God's glory. I want to suggest that, in some contexts, it is possible for public education to provide unique opportunities for Christian children to develop a biblical worldview, apologetic skills, and a passion for the Great Commission that simply cannot occur through Christian schooling or homeschooling.

Preparing to Make Your Choice

"There is," Paul wrote to the Christians in Rome, "no authority except from God, and those that exist are instituted by God" (Rom 13:1). Just as God is sovereign over the political systems in our country, He is also sovereign over the public schooling systems. That does not mean that everything is going well with public schooling. It *does* mean that God is greater than the problems in public schools. If your family is called to send children to public school, God will use public schooling for His glory.

So what should you do as you move toward the best choice for your child's education? Here are five suggestions:

1. Entrust your child's education to God. Formal instruction is not everything. Even if your child attends public school, more lifelong learning occurs in your home than in the school. Several years ago, I sat with the parent of a youth from the student ministry that I led at the time. This father was a successful businessman with three children; he was also a faithful Christian. As his oldest child approached high school, he and his wife decided to move their daughter from Christian school to public school. When I asked him how he knew what school was right for his daughter, he said, "Your goal must be to provide the best education you possibly can with the resources that are available to you." This man clearly could afford any school he wanted for his kids. Yet, as I continued to converse with him, I realized he knew that, regardless of what school his child attended, the most important learning occurred at home. That is the point of Deuteronomy 6:7–9. God's design is for learning and discipleship to be woven into every aspect of family life—into everything from vacations to chores, from academics to sports, from rising in the morning to tumbling into bed at night.

Such habits of life require persistent, specific prayer. Our older daughter faced several difficulties in fourth grade. Classmates were disruptive and disrespectful. Maddie consistently came home frustrated and concerned. One night, with tears in her eyes, she asked, "Why do they have to be so rude? I just want to learn. Why don't they want to learn too?" We began to pray by name for the students in her class and for her teacher. We shared her concerns with the teacher and even told the teacher that we were praying for him. Despite the teacher's best efforts, the disruptions continued throughout the year. Yet, in the midst of the disruptions, our daughter learned to rely on God to walk with her through a difficult time. She learned how to work with difficult people. She learned through habits of prayer at home that even if her circumstances did not change, she could choose to do what was right. That's what it means to entrust your child's education to God.

2. Never forget that every parent is called to homeschool. No, that is not a typo, and no, you have not accidentally flipped to the wrong chapter. Even if your child attends public school, you are responsible to homeschool and to *disciple your child personally.* There is no substitute for your influence and instruction in your child's life.

It is not the Sunday school teacher's task to equip your children to serve Jesus Christ. It is not even your pastor's job. You as a parent have been specifically commanded by God to embrace the task of discipling your children. You possess the primary responsibility for developing a biblical worldview in your child. To be sure, your church should partner with you in this task, but if your church is not equipping parents to disciple their own children, you and your church are both falling short of your God-ordained responsibilities. If you send your children to public school and do not personally disciple them, they will develop the same ethics and beliefs as the world around them. But that is not the fault of what school you chose! It is because you as a parent failed in your God-given role as the primary discipler of your children.

Discipling your children begins with the consistent practice of family devotions. In our household, it is non-negotiable that everyone arrives in the living room at 7:00 AM on school days. The curriculum is simple: We read from Psalms and Proverbs, and then we pray for specific concerns at school and for at least one friend who is not a Christian. Getting everyone into the living room no later than 7:00 AM is not easy, but this simple commitment helps us to focus on how God has called our family to reflect His image in public school. Even if you send your child to Christian school, you are responsible in the context of your family to train your child in a biblical worldview. If God calls you to send your child to public school, this training at home is not simply an academic exercise; it is real-life training for real-time challenges to biblical ethics and beliefs.

Real-life, real-time training does not end with daily devotions, though. Several years ago, my wife began intentionally teaching our older daughter about modesty. What made the principles really come alive was when they went shopping at the mall. (What pre-teen girl would not want to make the mall her classroom?) As my wife and daughter walked through the mall, they observed the clothes on the mannequins and discussed whether these clothing options matched up with biblical principles. The environment served to clarify the lessons learned through the discussion. That is what can happen when parents called of God send well-discipled children to public school: Because the environment includes real-life challenges, the environment serves to clarify the lessons.

3. Serve your school. Take every conceivable opportunity to invest in the administration, faculty, staff, and students by serving them. I am not talking about gaining access to the school so that you can criticize what is broken. Neither am I describing covert observations and operations so you can change the chosen methods or curriculum. Neither is this an opportunity to hover over your children. What I am suggesting is simply that you serve the school, with no strings attached. Servant-hearted volunteerism speaks volumes to skeptical staff members, and such an attitude can earn the right to be heard in the school system.

Since the moment our older daughter was enrolled in public school, my wife has volunteered at the school. She has made photocopies, dusted, re-shelved library books, and helped in dozens of other ways. During that time, Karla has earned the trust of many parents and educators. Not everyone shares our worldview, but Karla's service has created a context of trust in which conversations about our worldview can occur freely. Our involvement testifies to a conscious effort to engage our culture instead of retreating from it.

In the past year, I have volunteered to help a group of children with math facts—and it made a difference in their success. It also gave me the chance to know students in my daughter's class. They saw me as a trustworthy adult and as a caring parent. As a direct result of helping children with math facts, the principal asked me to serve on the Parent Advisory Council that meets monthly with the school superintendent. My wife was privileged to spend time in prayer with the president of the PAC. Can you see the potential impact here? Because of our efforts to serve the local public school, Christian parents now have a voice in shaping the educational environment of every child in this community. How could such an influence have occurred if we had decided to abandon our local public school?

My wife was also asked to serve as a parent reviewer when the school adopted new reading, writing, and spelling curricula. Public school curriculum is a battleground for cultural conflict, and it is a battlefield from which we refuse to retreat. By investing ourselves as servants of our school system, God has provided opportunities for us to have an impact on the curriculum used in our public school.

4. Network with believing teachers, staff, and parents. As we wrestled with the initial decision to send our daughter to public school, my wife and I visited the school to observe the facility and to meet the principal. During the visit, my wife briefly observed a first-grade classroom. That next Sunday, she pointed out a young woman in church who was the same first-grade teacher she saw the previous week! God used that moment to catalyze the calling to become involved in public schooling. It was a reminder of how many committed believers faithfully serve in the public school system. Remarkably, that same woman became my daughter's first-grade teacher. Since that time, we have discovered many other committed, Christian teachers.

Our younger daughter Katie has a strong sense of what she wants, but she becomes easily frustrated. Getting dressed often presents a challenge. One particularly difficult morning, she was unable to push past the frustration, and she was late to school. When she and my wife Karla arrived at school, Katie remained visibly upset. As Karla and Katie walked into the classroom, Karla motioned for her teacher and quietly explained that it had been a rough morning. Later, the teacher shared with my wife that she had approached our daughter and asked her if she was okay; then, she placed her hand on my daughter's shoulder and prayed for her during the moment of silence that our school observes each morning. My wife was able to share with our daughter that her teacher had prayed for her. In this way, Katie glimpsed faith in action inside a public school.

When our oldest daughter Maddie started second grade, we learned that her teacher was a Christian man, involved in a local church. During our first parent-teacher conference, we discovered that he and his wife attended the same church we did! Shortly after that meeting, they joined a Bible class that I taught. Several years later, he and his wife are committed to a church planting effort in our area, and he serves as a deacon. He and his wife remain influential people in both of our children's lives. This same teacher begins each school year by praying by name for each student before they arrive on the first day of school. The more we have immersed ourselves in our local public school, the more we have seen how God has stationed His people in this strategic arena.

As you network with Christians in your school, look for ways that you and your fellow-Christians can serve other families in the school, especially "the orphans and widows" (James 1:27)—families and children disadvantaged through death, divorce, or uncaring parents. As you see the needs, you can either be appalled by the plight of these people, or you can search for opportunities to serve them.

5. Be a Christian witness in your conversation and communication. This could be the most critical point of this chapter. Getting your Christian witness wrong will instantly confound your capacity to impact public schools in any positive way. Avoid the run-of-the-mill gossip at the Parent-Teacher Association (PTA) meetings. If adjustments do need to be made in your child's curriculum or context, follow the appropriate chains of command. The problem is *not* that you will sometimes need to address specific concerns with the school, because you will. The problem is whether you do so in a way that honors God. Scripture provides clear guidelines for how to approach conflict and for how to respect authority (Matt 18:12–20; Rom 13:1–10). Unless the public school is asking our family to dishonor God, we must respect the authority of the local public school. In doing so, we are responding to God's authority in our lives, as we can see in Romans, chapter 13.

Part of being a Christian witness includes assuming the best about the school's faculty, staff, and administration (see 1 Cor 13:7). There are many public-school educators who possess active and living faith in Jesus, and though they cannot openly express this faith, their belief remains even in the classroom. Their character and commitment can provide excellent examples for your children.

Parents as Primary Teachers

To give you a biblical reference point for your decision about your child's schooling, take a look at early biblical history to see how God instructed His people. One of the earliest recipients of God's teaching was Elihu, one of Job's acquaintances. Elihu listened to Job's ranting and became angry with him "because he had justified himself rather than God" (Job 32:2). Three times Elihu references God as our teacher (Job 33:16; 35:11; 36:22). There is no mention of school or any other system of education, just God as our teacher. What we see here is that education is not primarily the formal time spent in the classroom. It can include interaction with divine truth in any and every part of life.

Throughout the Hebrew Scriptures, it is clear that the primary instruction in children's lives comes through interaction with parents. One responsibility that God required from Abraham was to "command his children and his house after him to keep the way of the LORD by doing what is right and just" (Gen 18:19). The apostle Paul informed the Galatian church that the Old Testament law "was our schoolmaster to bring us unto Christ, that we may be justified" (Gal 3:24, KJV). And how was this law learned? Primarily, through the parents. The seventy-eighth psalm puts it this way:

> He established a testimony in Jacob and set up a law in Israel, which He commanded our fathers to teach to their children so that a future generation—children yet to be born—might know. They were to rise and tell their children so that they might put their confidence in God and not forget God's works, but keep His commandments. (5–7)

Parents taught by example (Deut 6:5–8; 31:12), through verbal communication (Deut 6:6–7; 11:18–19), through informal discussions (Deut 6:7; 11:19), by answering their children's questions in ways that called attention to God's glory (Exod 12:26; 13:14; Deut 6:20–21), through object lessons (Deut 6:9; 11:20), and by participating together in worship (Deut 16:16). Even after Hebrew parents in some areas began to send children to synagogue schools around the sixth century BC, the parents were still perceived as the primary educators in their children's lives.

What is my point in this?

If you are a parent, the education of your child is what matters most. Formal education is not everything. And especially as a public-school parent, it is your responsibility to train your children to view everything they learn in relation to a biblical worldview. That is what God intended from the beginning, regardless of your context. In contemporary society, this is especially true when it comes to science and history. These moments of learning become teachable moments for you as the parent when you help your child to view every part of life from the perspective of God's Word. Public-school parenting requires the greatest intentionality in this regard.

You cannot expect that your children will gain everything that they need to know about a Christian worldview simply by growing up in your home or by going to church. You are responsible to train them in this worldview, using Scripture alongside their school curriculum to move them toward Christ-centered thinking about every area of life.

Criticisms of Public Schooling

There are two primary and legitimate criticisms of public schools: *poor educational quality* and *exposure of children to worldly attitudes and behaviors.* Let us look together at the foundations for each of these criticisms.

Exposure to Ungodliness? Sheltering your child should never be a priority. Jesus told His followers to expect persecution, rejection, trials, and testing (Matt 5:10–12). Our family has chosen public school, in part, to provide our children with a relatively safe context where they can learn to deal with persecution and testing. We are providing real-time, real-life opportunities to apply what we have taught them. In this way, their faith is strengthened.

It would be absurd for a basketball team to practice for years without playing a game. It is equally absurd for children to train for years to follow Jesus without placing them in contexts where they are challenged in any significant, real-life ways. I am not saying that our children are ready to "play in the pros," so to speak, but they *are* experiencing consistent challenges that force them to live what they have learned at home. They are learning in a real-life context how to reflect the image of Christ in dark circumstances.

Put in the simplest possible terms, shelter and safety should not be our priority as Christian parents. "Making safety the priority tells our children that we think God is incapable of doing what he said he would do for his children."[3] Sin surrounds our children throughout their lives. A parent can modify behaviors for long periods of time by limiting the child's exposure to "the world." Eventually, however, children must have the opportunity to submit their wills personally to God and to witness His sovereignty in the world. Jesus said, "You will have suffering in this world. Be courageous! I have conquered the world" (John 16:33). If all Christians segregate their children in homeschools or covenantal Christian schools, can they really claim that they are "courageous" or that they are teaching our children that Jesus has already "conquered the world"? Can they state with confidence that they have gone "into the world" at all (John 17:16–18)?

Poor Educational Quality? One of the most common criticisms of the public school revolves around academic performance. E. Roy Moore has claimed, for example, that despite attending the best-funded schools in the world, American students rank near the bottom in math, science, and physics.[4] This is a driving impetus for what he has called "the Exodus Mandate"— the supposed responsibility for all Christians to remove their children from public schools.

Statistics are not telling us the whole story. I agree that public schools in the United States can and should improve. Yet, when we compare academic achievements in public schools with Christian schools and homeschools, it is important that we compare in *categorical equivalents* instead of *categorical generalities*. What I mean is that in American public schools, every child is tested. Because American schools are so diverse, test scores include children from middle-class, suburban, two-parent families as well as children whose families have only been in the United States for a few weeks, children whose kitchens do double-duty as methamphetamine labs, and children with undiagnosed learning disabilities. The diversity of American public schooling skews the statistics downward. Neither homeschooling nor Christian

---

3. T. Kimmel, *Grace-Based Parenting* (Nashville, Tenn.: W Publishers/Thomas Nelson, 2004), 116.
4. E. R. Moore, *Let My People Go* (Greenville, S.C.: Ambassador-Emerald, 2002), *passim*.

schooling includes the same breadth of diversity as American public schooling. For that matter, few other nations in the world encompass the same diversity in their schools as American public schools.

With that in mind, what are the educational realities when true categorical equivalents are compared? Here is how Paul Fahri summarized the real situation:

> No nation included in the major rankings educates more poor students or as ethnically diverse a population as does the U.S. When compared with students in the world's most industrialized nations, U.S. students were on par with the others. . . . Every Western country, not just the U.S., lagged behind Japan in math and science. The issue of academic achievement is not an exclusive American one, but a global, east-west one.[5]

In the end, Christian parents are responsible to secure the best education possible with the resources that God has given them. In many public school systems, it is entirely possible to achieve excellence in education.

This reality raises another concern. If it is possible for your family to be involved in your local public school without compromising your faith or your child's education, is Christian schooling or homeschooling truly a wise investment? If you are a resident of the United States of America, you are already investing in your local public school through your taxes. Materials for homeschooling can range from a few hundred extra dollars each year to several thousand. Christian school tuition in some areas exceeds ten thousand dollars per academic year. Suppose that these sums were invested in local missions, relieving financial stresses on fractured families whose children attend public schools. What impact could such investments have on the kingdom of God?

---

5. P. Fahri, "Five Myths about U.S. Kids, Outclassed by the Rest of the World," *The Washington Post* (January 21, 2007), B-02.

Public on Purpose and the Priority
of the Great Commission

Ultimately, for our family, this issue is about how we have been called to carry out the Great Commission. This does *not* mean that I am expecting my children to serve as full-time missionaries at school. I have friends who contend that they send their children to public schools as missionaries. I respectfully disagree with such a strategy. My children's calling is *not* to be campus evangelists or missionaries; they are young believers who are being equipped at home to carry their faith with them through their attitudes, behavior, and speech.

The kindness and gentleness of our daughter Maddie has a tremendous influence on her friends. She shares her faith through the ways that she responds to others. But I do not expect her to be a missionary. My wife and I are the missionaries, not our children. That calling will gradually—and prayerfully!—pass to our children as they mature and grow. Yet, as David and Kelli Pritchard have pointed out, "the main job for a Christian child or teenager in public school is simply to be a good student, a good citizen, and a servant-leader—to model what Christianity actually is."[6]

Climbing in with Them

When each of my girls was about eight months old, I began to teach them to swim. As a teenager, I worked one summer as an infant swimming instructor. So when I had children of my own, it was only natural for me to teach them to swim.

The process for teaching babies to swim was very simple. The mothers climbed into the pool with their babies and held them close as they moved around the shallow end. This continued for several weeks, and new skills were added one by one. The goal of this phase was simply to help infants overcome their fear of the pool. After a few weeks, I took mothers and babies to the deep

---

6. D. Pritchard and K. Pritchard, *Going Public* (Ventura, Calif.: Regal, 2008), 191–92.

end. We climbed in together, then floated or treaded water—but we never let the babies go.

Ultimately, the infants needed two opportunities to succeed: First, they needed to know that their mothers would be there for them. Even when we began to put distance between mothers and babies, the children needed to see that Mom was there for them. Second, the children needed the chance to try new skills. Not every infant was instantly agreeable in the water, and some children took longer to recognize that everything would be okay. Eventually, though, even these children learned to tread in deep water—but this required the parents to let go of the child while still remaining near.

If you conclude that God's calling for your family includes public school, let me provide one last encouragement: *Get in the water with your children.* You cannot simply choose a school, enroll your child, and walk away. You cannot entrust your child's worldview to the public school. You must release them to try new skills, but never at the cost of sacrificing their educational development to a secular school system. They are not ready to go it alone, but with the knowledge that you are there for them and with training at home, they can tread waters far deeper than you may expect.

Not every Christian family is called to public schooling, and public schooling is not a viable option in every place. Yet, for us and for many other Christian families, it is a divine calling that allows us to reflect God's light in a dark place.

CHAPTER 2

What Are the Problems with Public Schooling?

Response by G. Tyler Fischer
Perspective of Open-Admission Christian Schooling

It is difficult to criticize such a well-written essay penned by a husband and wife who have tried to take the Great Commission to heart. I salute the courage that their family has demonstrated by attempting to be Christian witnesses in their community. I was raised in similar circumstances, with godly parents working to serve the public school and to counteract the training that I received there. Remembering that experience, I agree with the advice given in the last chapter for parents who do choose to send children to public school. The commitment to be involved in the life of a local community is also healthy. And I praise their rejection of the claim that "my kids are missionaries"! With the recognition in this chapter that parents—not children—are the missionaries, I hope that the notion of children as missionaries has finally been put to rest. Thus far, applause!

I have three primary objections to the claims made by Troy and Karla Temple. First, there is a lack of imagination. Throughout their chapter, there seems to be an undercurrent that whispers, "Look what parents can do to undo a public school education!" While the motivation may be laudable, imagine with me

Now subscribe online at
archdigest.com/orderF21

First issue mails within 4 weeks.
Please add applicable sales tax.

BUSINESS REPLY MAIL

FIRST-CLASS MAIL   PERMIT NO. 107   BOONE IA

POSTAGE WILL BE PAID BY ADDRESSEE

ARCHITECTURAL DIGEST

PO BOX 37617
BOONE IA 50037-2617

what could happen if schoolteachers, parents, and pastors were all working together to develop children into disciples of Jesus Christ. Imagine what a child could be taught if Christian public school parents took the time they spend undoing public schooling and invested it in building the child's knowledge and character in partnership with a Christian school!

Second, in other places, there is an overuse of imagination. There is, for example, the suggestion that, "If you are a resident of the United States of America, you are already investing in your local public school through your taxes. . . . What impact could such investments have on the kingdom of God?" Somehow, I do not identify being required to sink money into a flawed and faulty educational system as "investing." Considering the track record of public schooling over the past century, this is an investment any sensible investor would have unloaded a long time ago. Furthermore, let's suppose that Christians actually *did* transfer their resources by quitting Christian education and giving to the poor. What would be the most effective venture that the poor could undertake with this money? It would probably be to get their children out of failed inner-city public schools and to place these children in quality schools such as the Christian schools we would have just dismantled!

The third and most crucial flaw I see in this chapter is the recommended remedy for the worldview problems in public education. The recommended remedy seems to be to pray with your children, to get involved in the public school, to build a support network, and to disciple your children personally. But such a strategy completely misses the main point. The secular worldview that has been entrenched in public education distorts and disfigures the entire educational process. To be sure, it is possible to learn reading, writing, and sums in a public school. Yet education is far broader than these basic skills. Education necessarily includes value judgments and answers to questions of "why." *Why* is there order rather than disorder? *Why* is it wrong to kill babies? *Why* is it wrong to lie on your taxes or to cheat on your tests? If a God-centered worldview is excluded, these questions cannot be sufficiently or honestly answered, and the entire educational process inevitably becomes substandard. Scripture makes it clear that "the fear of the LORD is the beginning of wisdom" (Prov 1:7); as such, without reference to God, authentic education cannot even begin. All wisdom and all reality are rooted in the character and identity of Jesus Christ. Education without Christ is not education at all but rather a charade.

The fix offered is utterly insufficient. Even if Christian parents fight back the condoms, the facile acceptance of homosexuality, and the assumption that evolution can explain our origins, what about all that is *not* taught? What about the truths that public schools must hide from? What about the glories of the Middle Ages that were inextricably intertwined with faith? What about the teachings of Christian philosophers that are ignored or gutted of their underlying motivations? What about the study of the Bible as a reliable historical text? Public schools cannot and will not touch these truths, and yet Christians know these truths are necessary for adequate education.

The Temples' use of Deuteronomy chapter 6 stretches the text far beyond its context. Would it be acceptable to send your children to an Islamic Madrasah as long as you corrected the damage each evening? What is taught in a public school is every bit as corrosive to a biblical worldview as what is taught in the most militant Madrasah in the Muslim world! Believing that parents are actually following the intent of Deuteronomy 6:7–9 when they send children to spend most of their waking hours in an environment that will not allow the name of Christ on any doorpost or gate badly misses the point of the biblical text. No self-respecting Israelite would have believed he was obeying the words of Moses while sending his child to Baal Secondary School or Learn Without Yahweh Academy. Why? Because they knew that God expected them to immerse their children in an environment of faith.

There is much to praise in the "Public on Purpose" chapter, but public schools have been and will continue to be dark places. The heart of this darkness dwells not primarily in drug deals or immorality or immodest dress, but in the underlying worldview of these schools. It is a worldview that necessarily and unavoidably cripples authentic Christian education.

Response by Mark Eckel
Perspective of Covenantal Christian Schooling

High marks go to these parents for their dedication to training children within the framework of a Christian home while working within the public school system. If only all Christian parents in their situation would be so dutiful! Still, I must cite two inevitable impediments to public education for Christian young people.

First, relational discipleship. In my many years of teaching, spending forty-five minutes a day, five days a week, one hundred and eighty days each year with my students had tremendous impact on students' future lives. Why? I was with them. I built relationships with them. They heard me, questioned me, watched me, laughed with me, and cried with me. They saw me at their games, plays, and recitals. They came to my home for parties. Relational discipleship seeks to make students imitators of one's person and belief (1 Thess 1:2–2:14). No public school teacher—even if he or she is a Christian—can do what teachers do in covenantal Christian schools.

Second, belief. Everyone believes something, and these beliefs will be taught. Every statement a teacher makes in class is born from some belief. Every belief impacts individuals and institutions, and no beliefs are neutral. Herein is my major objection to public schooling for Christian children.

For the Hebrew, everything was theological. Everything pointed back to God. Behavior was based on belief for generations to come (Exod 12:42). For Old Testament believers, teaching the meaning of everything was a God-centered practice. A Christian school can respond in obedience to these divine demands. A public school cannot.

Promoting a biblical heritage necessitates the recognition that there is no neutrality in education. A teacher's intention will be displayed through choices in curriculum, words, and attitudes. The teacher conveys importance to certain aspects of study, and what the teacher deems important may not reflect the parents' belief system. A teacher's instruction, including their views of children, authority, and educational philosophy, is determined by personal biases and beliefs. A Christian school can establish Christian principles for these arenas of life. A public school cannot.

Passing belief from one generation to another is mandated by Scripture (Ps 71:14–18; 78:1–8), and the responsibility of education ultimately rests on the bond that God established between parent and child. Where and with whom children spend the bulk of their day in school is one of the most important decisions a parent will ever make. A Christian school can provide partnership with Christian parents who desire biblically-based education. A public school cannot.

Response by Michael S. Wilder
Perspective of Homeschooling

I want to begin my response to this chapter by stating what I appreciate about the argument. Troy initiates the conversation by admitting that not every Christian parent should send children to public school. For those who do, it should be a divine calling. The underlying principle that surfaces here is the wise recognition that Christian parents must have a deliberate process in place as they consider their educational options. I am convinced most Christian parents today fail to ask the right educational questions, to the detriment of their families.

I also appreciate the balanced approach Troy demonstrates when he addresses the variations in quality and culture in public schools. Some public schools are so large and the secular influences are so pervasive that a Christian parent's presence and protests will never be noticed. He suggests in these situations that Christian parents *not* include public schooling in their list of options.

Still, I must pose some questions: What public school will ever be an appropriate educational partner? What public school system, no matter how involved Christian parents may become, will ever integrate faith with learning? What public school system will ever exhibit a Christian values system?

The answer is not complicated.

The answer is *none.*

As the chapter on sending our children to public school points out, the goal is *not* success in life but the reflection of God's glory. The author is accurate in suggesting that the goal is indeed conformity to the image of Jesus Christ. Yet, if one truly believes that education is a part of the larger life-discipleship process, and if we recognize that children spend 30 percent of their waking hours in a schooling environment, I am confused why anyone would advocate placing young believers in an anti-Christian context as a means to move them toward maturity in Christ. Troy even acknowledges that children are at a real risk of developing "the same ethics and beliefs as the world around them" if their parents do not proactively disciple them. I contend that one part of proactive discipleship ought to be placing our children in educational contexts in which all subjects are taught in a way that reflects a biblical worldview.

It is true that, when our children face difficulties and opposing views, they can grow through processes of cognitive dissonance and resolution. As such, I agree that children *could* spiritually mature in a public school. Yet, if the goal is conformity to the character of Christ and reflection of God's glory, how much more could a Christian educational environment spur growth? Much more, I would contend.

Another major weakness in defending public schooling is the apparent failure to consider the educational philosophies that drive most secular educational systems. Examine the last three decades of public schooling, and you will see a systematic movement toward an educational philosophy that is known as *essentialism.*

The previous dominant educational philosophy was *progressivism.* Progressivism had been child-centered in its educational approach. Essentialism responded to progressivism, arguing that progressivism was destroying the intellectual fabric of America by abandoning the need for students to master educational basics. Essentialism arose in the 1930s but gained momentum in the 1970s and 1980s as the federal government imposed graduation standards in public schools. Essentialism became even more entrenched in the public schools when the No Child Left Behind Act became law in 2002.

I agree that there is essential knowledge students must gain. Yet the total focus of essentialism on cognitive development—to the exclusion of any concern for the affective, spiritual, or physical development of the student—concerns me. Because of essentialism, public schools have virtually rejected any educational approaches that develop the whole person. Christian parents must recognize that public school children will typically spend one-third of their waking hours with teachers whose primary concern is cognitive development. If education is truly a subset of discipleship—as I argue in my chapter—I am not convinced that public schools can provide a context where Christians should place their children.

I also take exception to implying that if we do not engage our culture by immersing ourselves in the public schools we are retreating from the culture. The author asks, "If all Christians segregate their children in homeschools or covenantal Christian schools, can they really claim they are courageous?" The connotation seems to be that those who *do not* place their children in public schools may refuse to do so because of cowardice. This statement seems to insinuate that the underlying motivation is to isolate children from harmful worldly influence.

My response to this is twofold: First, many parents opt out of public education for reasons other than worldly influences. Some of these parents are ideologically motivated, some are pedagogically motivated, while others are concerned about lifestyle factors. It is unfair to suggest that all parents remove their children because of environmental concerns. Second, I would ask if we are isolating our children from the world or if we are actually preparing them to minister to the world. Perhaps some parents *are* isolating their children, but many parents remove their children from public schools so they can strengthen and prepare their children to minister to the world.

Let's look last of all at the idea that Christian parents ought to use their children's enrollment in public school as a means of advancing the gospel. In this argument, the author places the primary responsibility for fulfilling the Great Commission on the parents, not on children. He emphatically states that the children "are not missionaries"; their responsibility is simply to live godly lives in their school setting. From this, it seems that he advocates public schooling based on missional opportunities for the parents instead of the educational and spiritual needs of the child. I suggest that it is not necessary for a Christian family to partner with a secular school to fulfill the Great Commission. There are many ways to obey the Great Commission without placing a child in a public school. The priority of the Great Commission should not preclude the priority of a child's educational and spiritual needs.

Counter-Response by Troy Temple
Perspective of Public Schooling

As I sit in this coffee shop considering the responses of my coauthors, I am so thankful that God has blessed His church with Christian thinkers who so deeply desire to see parents carry out their God-given mission. I appreciate their responses, and I know that all of us ultimately long to see Jesus lifted up so that He will draw people to Himself.

God has appointed a purpose for every life. It is described in the twelfth chapter of Genesis, when Abraham enters into a covenant with God. That covenant involved a promise that God would bless Abraham, that Abraham's seed would become a great nation, and that Abraham's name would grow great. But that is only half the promise. Abraham was told that he would *be blessed* so that he would *be a blessing*. God has saved us so we will be on the offensive for His gospel and for the Messiah.

Our choice to send our children to public school is related to nothing less than our obedient response to what God has confirmed in our hearts for us to do. This is how God has called us to be a blessing to the world around us. As I have said before, public school is not for every Christian family, but the sole effective remedy for the worldview problems in the public school is not retreat but the gospel itself. The applied message of salvation can change anything and everything, even the culture of a public school.

Whatever option your family chooses for your children's education, the choice must be made with great intentionality. My fellow contributors give you three great choices for educating your children, but none of them will be effective if you fail to disciple your own children, and neither will public schooling. Regardless of where your child attends school, God has called you as a believing parent to disciple your children.

A critical error in the contemporary Christian family has been the casual approach to discipling children that surrenders the children's discipleship to church leadership or to a Christian school. God did not call Christian schools to make disciples. While Christian schools may be led by believers, the Christian school is not an institution that Scripture mandates.

Homeschooling does seek to locate the comprehensive care and training of children in the initial institution found in Scripture, the family. Homeschooling is an intensely deliberate choice that does seem to counteract the abdication of parents' role that can occur in Christian schooling, as well as in many contemporary churches' approach to children and adolescents. While I agree that it may be a cleaner option for coordinated academic and Christian education, I see so many areas where parents must enter it with eyes wide open.

Regardless of where God leads your family, do not surrender your role as a parent or take lightly your responsibility to shepherd the gift God has given you in your child. Be intentional in your choice, and be actively involved in the process. You will be the one who gives an account for your child's education, not anyone else. Choose wisely, enjoy the journey, and seek God's best for *your* family.

CHAPTER 3

Christian Schooling for Everyone

HOW OPEN-ADMISSION CHRISTIAN SCHOOLS IMPACT THE WORLD

By G. Tyler Fischer

"You're kidding," I said. "You're sure that's where he's going?"

"That's what they said," my executive assistant replied. "Mr. Stolzfus leaves in a couple hours."

I knew that this opportunity might never come again. A father connected to our school was leaving on a trip that would take him near one of the most exciting, and perhaps most important, Christian schools in the world. I had heard a lot about the leaders and students at this school, and I wanted to introduce our school to them.

I called an impromptu staff meeting. Calls were made, information was assembled, items were purchased and packaged. Someone was even dispatched to get a bag of Wilbur Buds—the superior version of Hershey Kisses that is a product of Lancaster County, Pennsylvania. After the treats and information were assembled, the father promised that he would do his best to locate the school once he arrived at his destination.

What was the point of this flurry of activity?

Simply this: We wanted to make a positive impression.

We wanted to make an impact.

All schooling makes an impact, but not every impression or impact is positive. In recent years, there has been a spate of movies dramatizing the effect a comet or asteroid might have if it impacted the Earth. It probably goes without saying that the results of such impacts would not be particularly pleasant. Some impacts can be disastrous.

I suggest that poor educational practices have an impact far more devastating than any intergalactic calamity that has ever shot across the silver screen. If the movies are to be believed, people would soon band together and rebuild if some celestial object impacted the Earth. When it comes to the effect of poor educational practices, it is far more difficult to see the craters that need filling and the structures that need rebuilding. Deficient education produces ongoing impacts far worse than Texas-sized holes in the earth. Poor schooling affects the way people perceive themselves, each other, their culture, and their world. The results of such education continue to wreak havoc long after any community would have gained the sense to rebuild.

The good news, however, is that education also holds great promise and great possibilities for positive impact. Think of the monastic schools in Europe in the Middle Ages, the educational philosophies of Jan Amos Comenius, the Methodist movement in England that probably kept that nation from lapsing into revolution. These educational practices made an impact, too—not gaping craters, but imprints of the character and nature of Jesus Christ.

That is the kind of impact that I hope to leave. I believe the best way to leave this sort of impact is through open-admission Christian schooling. In open-admission Christian schools, students from every background are potentially eligible for admission. While maintaining a Christ-centered curriculum, open-admission Christian schools do not require that students come from Christian families. Open-admission Christian schooling gives freedom to the school's administrators to act in the best interest of the students and families by admitting students who will aid the school in fulfilling its vision. This vision includes educating not only students from Christian homes, but also students whose families may not be Christians at all. Because of the strong possibility that God may use open-admission Christian schools to bring non-Christians to salvation, these schools are sometimes known as "evangelistic Christian schools" or "missional Christian schools."

How Open-Admission Schooling Works

Before discussing why open-admission Christian schooling is the best option, let's look at how these schools work. Open-admission schools work most effectively when an admissions committee is empowered to act in the school's best interest when deciding whom to admit. It is absolutely essential that this committee make the necessary choices, even if these choices are unpopular, to move toward the school's central vision.

Such a committee must embrace three vital tasks: First, the admissions committee needs to be clear about what is in the school's best interest. The first priority for an admissions committee must be to admit students and families who will help the school maintain its mission and fulfill its vision. This—not money or growth—is the most important matter for the admissions committee.

Second, having a clear mission and vision, however, is not the only critical matter. Being on an admissions committee requires backbone! Allow me to state the matter bluntly: This committee must be willing to say no to the pastor's daughter or to the donor's son if this child's presence might hamper the school's fulfillment of its mission. A few poor decisions can do for a school what a single rotten egg will do for an omelet.

Third, it is also necessary to consider what steps must be taken to ensure that the admissions committee has sufficient information to make the best decisions. To be sure, records from previous schools should be consulted. Yet admissions decisions cannot be based on transcripts alone. Face-to-face interactions with families and students are necessary too.

I work at a classical Christian school where every new student takes a placement test. While the student takes this test, one or more school administrators or board members meet the prospective family.[1] During this test, an administrator may speak with the family about what the school believes and what the school teaches. This administrator also listens to the family for the purpose of providing a helpful report about the family to the admissions committee. The family also has opportunities during this time to ask questions about the school.

It is during this time that a careful administrator must consider three keys to admission. These three keys are the *key of comfort, the key of company,* and *the key of commitment.* Together, these keys can tell whether the student and the school are compatible.

The Key of Comfort: Is the Family Comfortable with the School's Expectations?

While interacting with the parents of a prospective student, every administrator must be transparent, seeking opportunities to help parents understand what the school expects and what the school will teach their child. This transparency is particularly important when dealing with unbelieving families or with families whose beliefs differ from the school's statement of faith. Parents must know what behavioral standards will be expected and maintained. Parents must also be aware of how the school approaches specific questions relating to faith and salvation.

At the classical school where I am privileged to work, parents of prospective students are informed that the school will train their child to think and to live like a Christian. Students are expected to act like believers in Jesus Christ while at school, and to maintain a lifestyle outside of school that is consistent with their life in school. They are expected to talk like believers in Jesus Christ, to submit to authority like believers, to work like believers, and to ask for forgiveness like believers, and this is true

---

1. Many open-admission Christian schools, including the one where I serve as headmaster, allow this meeting to occur with the parents and only one administrator. It is optimal, however, to have two persons in the room with the family. Also, it is critical that both parents are present. If a schooling decision is not important enough for parents to take a couple hours off work, these are probably not the type of parents that will help the school to fulfill its mission.

even if they are not believers. If parents support these expectations, their child will probably fit well in the school. If parents do not support such expectations, their child does not belong in our school. If the family and the school cannot "turn the key of comfort," the school cannot engage in education *in loco parentis*—that is to say, with authority over the child that has been delegated to the school by the parents.[2]

Administrators will reap great benefits by being blunt with potential parents. Pressing the point will help the administrator to recognize whether the family's comfort level goes further than nodding acquiescence. Administrators should inform prospective families that the school will be teaching their child that salvation is found only in Jesus Christ. While a non-Christian family might initially nod their consent, the administrator would be wise to ask the family how they will feel if their son or daughter comes home and draws the obvious implication that unless Mommy and Daddy trust Jesus Christ, they are condemned before God. If a school is committed to a particular set of doctrines or practices, a school must be open and honest with parents about this. In some instances, this may mean that good Christian families go elsewhere.

Another potential issue involves how the school will teach children to view matters like marriage and divorce. A school committed to a biblical worldview must speak about these matters from a biblical perspective. Is this family prepared to accept the fact that their child will be presented with a biblical worldview in this area of life? Give the parents as clear a picture as possible. If they are not prepared to accept the school's teachings in matters of this sort, do not admit their child.

The Key of Company: Is the School Maintaining a Wise Balance?

The next key is the key of company. Even if unbelieving parents are comfortable with the school and the school is

---

2. *In loco parentis* is a Latin phrase meaning "in the place of the parents." It means that the school does the work of education under authority delegated not by the state or by the church but by the parents. Parents can only delegate well and knowledgeably if they know what their child will be learning.

comfortable with the parents, admitting their child might not be a wise choice. Remember what the apostle Paul said? "Bad company corrupts good character" (1 Cor 15:33). Admitting one or two unbelieving students in a grade filled with believing students from strong families is one thing. Admitting the fifth student from a non-Christian family into a class of twenty is quite another. It is crucial to maintain a balance of students and personalities that insures Christian leadership within a class. The wrong mix of students can turn a Christian environment upside down.

Another consideration is that the older the student applying for admission is, the more the admissions committee ought to beware. To be sure, every child is sinful, but age, experience, and practice can turn a mildly annoying child into a recklessly dangerous teenager—perhaps even a recklessly dangerous teenager who seems to an admissions committee like an angel of light. When considering an older student from an unbelieving family, a committee must give careful attention to the present make-up of the class. Is there strong and righteous leadership among students in this class? If a particular student might bring a lack of balance to the class, do not admit the student, even if he is the best basketball player in the county, or if she is the daughter of the pastor of the largest church in town.

The Key of Commitment: Will the Student Carry Through?

If the admissions committee and family have turned the keys of comfort and company, that leaves only one more key—the key of commitment. This key is particularly important for students in middle school and high school. Especially in the older grades, a student must be personally on-board with the work and with the commitments that are expected. At this point, the attitude of the student is fundamental.

Normally, this commitment will become evident as students consider the difficult work they will have to do to catch up academically. A high commitment level is a great sign that the student is ready for admission. Older students can make incredible strides when they set their minds to it. They might make up five years of math in a single summer or personally earn the money to pay for Latin tutoring! These are the sorts of actions that suggest maturity and high levels of commitment.

What an Open-Admission Christian School Must Not Do

Many otherwise Christian schools have rejected the open-admission approach in favor of stricter options, such as limiting enrollment to students from Christian homes. I believe that the decision against an open admission is typically made because the school does not understand what an open-admission policy really means. Sometimes, this misunderstanding occurs because parents or administrators have had bad experiences with poorly-managed open-admission schools.

Please allow me to make this point clearly: I do not mean by "open-admission" that the school should uncritically admit every student. What I mean is that Christian schools should consciously and carefully admit both believers and non-believers with the goal of being a witness to non-believers and of training all people to think theologically about education. A school that freely admits students on a "first come, first served" basis can potentially lose control of its environment and thereby forfeit a distinctively Christian education. Well-ordered admissions policies avoid these pitfalls. The school controls the composition of its student body by selecting students, whether Christian or non-Christian, whose enrollment is in the best interest of the academy and its families.[3]

To say it bluntly, schools that enroll bad students should not blame open-admission Christian schooling for their problem; the school should take the blame for having made poor admissions decisions. If a godly educational context is precious and important—and I believe that it is—it must be guarded. This guardianship is best accomplished through careful policies that are executed by committees and individuals who act in the

---

3. In the past, the school that I serve has maintained both an open-admission approach and a "first come, first served" method of selection. In Lancaster County, where the majority of families are Christian, this approach has not harmed the school. As I write, however, our board is considering moving away from a "first come, first served" approach.

school's best interests. Such guardianship includes care not only when admitting students but also when appointing students or parents to positions of leadership. If a godly and gutsy admissions committee works with godly and gutsy administrators to enforce wise and well-written admissions policies—structured around the keys of comfort, company, and commitment—the open-admission school will be equipped to make a maximum impact for Christ in the world.

Why Open-Admission Christian Schools Have the Greatest Impact

As I look at the different educational options available to Christian families, I am convinced that open-admission Christian schooling provides the greatest positive potential for making an impact for Jesus Christ. With that in mind, let's look at the other options—public school, homeschooling, and covenantal Christian schooling—to see where and why they fall short.

The Impact of Public Education

First, let me lay my cards on the table: *I do not believe that Christian families should send their children to public schools. For that matter, I do not think that non-Christian families should send their children to public schools either!* I am convinced that public education as it is presently organized and implemented in Western culture is a bad idea.

By saying this, please note that I am arguing against *institutions and ideas*—not against *people*. Throughout public school systems, there are intelligent and well-intended educators, administrators, board members, and parents. Some of these people are my friends and family members. I stand in awe of the sacrifices that they make, and I sympathize with their struggles. These people are positively influencing students, co-workers, and communities. I applaud their motives and their efforts. Each day, they strive to honor Jesus Christ in the shadow of a frustrating system, one that demands they make good citizens without mentioning the Creator who endows us with inalienable rights, that they produce smart students without being able to tell students that God has called them to study, and that they produce well-disciplined students in an environment that excludes any reference to absolute truth. They are ordered to make bricks without straw. Still, they persist in the face of staggering odds because they love the students and families that they serve. The efforts of these good women and men may be the sole factors that have prevented the complete collapse of the present public system.

I also recognize that many families feel trapped in a system of public schooling because they do not believe they possess the financial resources to leave. Still, I stand by my assertion that neither Christian nor non-Christian families should send their children to public schools. Christian families should not send their children to public schools because these schools fail to recognize that all education is theological. The central theological statement in the Hebrew Scriptures was, ultimately, a statement about education:

> Listen, Israel: The LORD our God, the LORD is One. Love the LORD your God with all your heart, with all your soul, and with all your strength. These words that I am giving you today are to be in your heart. Repeat them to your children. Talk about them when you sit in your house and when you walk along the road, when you lie down and when you get up. Bind them as a sign on your hand and let them be a symbol on your forehead. Write them on the doorposts of your house and on your gates. (Deut 6:4–9)

Similarly, in the New Testament, God's directive to fathers is educational. Notice the terms *training* and *instruction* in this text:

> Fathers, don't stir up anger in your children, but bring them up in the training and instruction of the Lord. (Eph 6:4)

The first passage is the famous *Shema*, which continually reminded the Israelites of their theological foundations. What is contained in this core statement of faith? Theological education, all the time—"when you sit . . . when you walk . . . when you lie down . . . when you rise up." If the point is not yet clear, the passage in Deuteronomy continues: "Bind them as a sign on your hand and . . . a symbol on your forehead . . . write them on the doorposts . . . and on your gates."

The environment that God commands believing parents to provide for their children is one in which the Word of God is part of each day's education—and not only as children learn about the Bible but also as children learn about every part of life, including academics. The passage in Ephesians commands parents to guide children in the "training and instruction" of the Lord. The Greek word for *nurture* or *training* is *paideia*. What this word implies is that Christian parents are called to cultivate constant patterns of faith in every part of life.[4]

This simply cannot occur in a public school. In some cases, children have been forbidden even to wear a Bible verse on their own t-shirts when in attendance at a public school! How can God's Word be bound upon our hearts, in every part of life, when it is excluded from consideration throughout the educational endeavor?

Why Public Schooling Has Failed

Over the past sixty years, a radical change has occurred in public school systems. For a century or so, from the advent of public schooling in the mid-1800s until the closing few decades of the twentieth century, American public schools may not have been explicitly religious, but they adhered to a sort of vague, non-sectarian Protestantism. Most Protestants seem to have been pleased with this arrangement. Since public schooling was not explicitly religious, Protestants also apparently felt few qualms about taking tax dollars from Roman Catholic families to run schools that generally presented Protestant beliefs and ethics. This insult, however, was not lost on Roman Catholics. The Roman Catholic parochial school system in the United States is a direct result of this disparity. Now, in some sense, the tables have been turned because the tax dollars of Protestant Christians are now siphoned off to provide children with an education

---

4. For more on this important passage see D. Wilson's book *The Paideia of God* (Moscow, Idaho: Canon, 1999). See also W. Bauer, et al., *A Greek-English Lexicon on the New Testament* (Chicago: University of Chicago Press, 1979), 603.

that presses secular beliefs and ethics while claiming to be irreligious.

The problem is that no school—public or religious—is "irreligious." Why? Because education is an unavoidably theological endeavor. By educating without reference to God, the public school declares implicitly that it is possible for a child to become a well-educated adult without any reference to God, to Jesus, or to absolute truth. This is a pernicious lie. It is pernicious because it is never openly stated or admitted. It is simply part of the educational air that children breathe in a public school. As a result, here is the basic message taught in public schools, in a slightly overstated form:

> You and the rest of the world are a cosmic accident. There is no ultimate purpose to life beyond making your personal existence more comfortable. You need this education to get a good job and have more stuff to fill your empty self. There's no ultimate meaning in life that I can tell you about. Nothing is absolutely right or wrong—but be good and do good things, whatever that means. The worst thing you can do is think that you are right about something or that someone else might be wrong. Our galaxy is eventually going to contract back into a rather tight spot; so, long-term investments—at least of the eternal and everlasting sort—may be problematic and impractical.

By avoiding religious references, the public school especially makes a mess of historical education, since religion is so deeply woven into history. Historical motivations that actually included religious impulses tend to be reduced to economics or mere pragmatism. Christian motivations for movements such as the abolition of slavery, women's suffrage, and civil rights are downplayed.

The mess does not end with historical education, however. Mathematical order is treated as the outgrowth of a randomly-generated universe, which just so happens to be able to support life, and scientific reliability rests on the subjective authority of scientists. If one cannot speak of God, nothing much makes sense in education.

To be sure, a few Christian families might declare that, with strong training at home and at church, their children can survive this poisonous miasma. But recent statistics expose this perspective as a delusion. A survey conducted by the Barna Group has revealed that only about 4 percent of the children of evangelicals—the majority of whom attend public schools—completely follow in their parents' footsteps of faith.[5] The problem is not, I suggest, that truth is not being provided to these children. The message is being provided, but the clamor of secularized education deafens these children to the voice of truth.

Some Christian families might declare that they remain in public schools because of a Great Commission impulse. They desire to be salt and light in a dark and tasteless world. I applaud this motive, so long as it is applied solely to those qualified to be missionaries in such pervasively secular environments. As such, if God has called a college-educated Christian adult to serve as a public school teacher or administrator and to provide Christian care and support in that context, I support that individual as a true missionary.

If families are expecting their children to serve as missionaries in such a context, however, I ask them to re-examine their thinking. Is a ten-year-old ready to be a missionary in a context where every aspect of education and socialization is implicitly required to exclude any reference to God? Of course not! In nearly all cases, the mission of secularism will triumph over the child's capacities to stand for truth.

The kind of education that God demands for His followers simply cannot occur in public school. But why should non-Christians avoid public schools? Simply because even non-Christian parents should not want their children to be trained in an incoherent worldview. The party line in our public schools

5. See, e.g., http://www.barna.org/FlexPage.aspx?Page=BarnaUpdates#2004. Also, one can find various perspectives online at http://www.pbs.org/newshour/generation-next/ demographic/religion3_11-21.html; for the atheist perspective, http://atheism.about .com/b/2006/10/21/evangelical-teens-leaving-the-faith-indroves.htm as well as http:// www.nytimes.com/2006/10/06/us/06evangelical.html?_r=1&pagewanted=2&hp&oref= slogin.

is a bad story to tell Christian children. It is also a bad story to tell to Jewish, Muslim, Buddhist, or Hindu children. It is a story line that leads to hopelessness, regardless of one's particular religious convictions.

The present public-education system fails to provide not only a coherent worldview but also an adequate education for many students. The staggering slide of public education is not difficult to document, but it is hard to keep up with. The Gates Foundation recently found that only 32 percent of public school graduates were academically prepared to attend a four-year college.[6] Colleges are responding to this trend by beefing up remedial classes and by lowering standards.[7] Math and science scores on standardized tests continue to spiral downward, leaving students continually less prepared to contribute to a community, to provide for their families, and to attain their aspirations.[8] Even if one takes into account that the American public-school system includes students from more diverse social and cultural strata than other nations, there is still cause for concern. Why? Because the academic quality of the American system has tended to decline year-by-year. If present trends continue, a child in a public elementary school today will receive a worse high-school education than high-school students are receiving right now.

Part of the problem is that the present public education system is cut off from market forces. This absence of market forces immunizes public education from what could be its greatest tutor. As the headmaster of a private school, I wake up each morning knowing that if I do a rotten job as an administrator, or if my teachers fail to provide a product that is worth the tuition, we will be forced to lower prices or to find new jobs. Families will— and should!—go somewhere else. This fact is a massive incentive that causes my teachers and staff to ask constantly how to do things better. This motive is missing in public education. The

---

6. See, e.g., http://www.renewamerica.us/columns/zeiger/040207.

7. See, e.g., http://www.usnews.com/blogs/paper-trail/2008/7/17/uc-discusses-radical-change-toadmissions.html.

8. See, e.g., http://www.centerforpubliceducation.org/site/c.kjJXJ5MPIwE/b.3642453/k.B171/US_15_yearolds_lag_in_math_and_science_on_international_test.htm and http://www.washingtonpost.com/wpdyn/content/article/2007/12/04/AR2007120400730.html.

introduction of market incentives would benefit taxpayers and help to raise the academic standards in public schools.

At this moment in history, American public schools are broken. Personally, I do not believe that they can ever be completely fixed. To fix them one would have to admit that all education is intrinsically religious. While I honor the Christian parents and teachers in public schools, I plead with all families to remove their children from them.

The Impact of Homeschooling

It is difficult to overestimate the potential positive impact of homeschooling. Its impact can be seen throughout the lives of students and parents. My school is very friendly with home-schooled families, even opening some classes to homeschoolers. When permitted by the regional athletic association, our sports teams play against their teams. For these reasons, I know that homeschooling can work.

Commenting on the impact of homeschooling is more difficult than commenting on public schooling, because there is no overarching, monolithic organization. As a result, the quality of homeschooling varies from family to family. In my experience, it typically follows a reversed bell curve: Families either do it very well or they do it very poorly, with very few in between. Many, I admit, do it well. Because so many homeschooling parents do teach their children at such high levels of excellence, I am perplexed by the high-handed persecution that I see them face from time to time. Homeschooling serves communities by reducing tax burdens and by bringing some market forces to bear on the public system—and perhaps this is the reason for the persecution. Homeschooling can result in an incredible education not only for some students but for some parents. I often meet mothers and fathers who have experienced an educational renaissance simply because they had to learn things in order to teach them to their children.

The positive impact of homeschooling is, however, limited in its scope and duration. Once your children are grown, any positive impact that can occur directly through your practice of home education is finished. Furthermore, homeschooling fails to take advantage of the principle of division of labor—the fact that God has gifted some persons to do certain tasks well and that we are best served when we allow those persons to do what God has called them to do.

The fact that not everyone knows every subject well makes homeschooling difficult for almost every parent at some point. I know of no parent who can teach Latin and Greek, Aquinas and Aristotle, calculus and chemistry, all at high levels of competence. I certainly can't. Yet there are Christian teachers that God has gifted in these areas. To the credit of homeschoolers, many form alliances ("cooperatives") with other families to compensate for these inevitable weaknesses. When this occurs, however, their practices begin to look a lot like a Christian school rather than a homeschool.

Another problem with homeschooling is that it is often motivated by retreat rather than vision, and it is no secret what parents are retreating from. Homeschoolers are retreating from the assumptions that evolution is the only possible explanation of our origins, that moral values are relative, and that their culture ought to embrace clothing and piercings that would have resulted in immediate expulsion from school a generation ago. Still, I am convinced that complete retreat can never revive or resuscitate a dying culture. The greatest impact becomes possible when parents are running toward a vision, not away from a villain.

Most important of all, homeschooling neglects the crucial truth that we are not merely members of families; we are members of communities, and our responsibilities as Christians and as citizens extend beyond our families. (This is one of the few areas—perhaps the only area—where public schooling actually gets something right.) Too often, as I interact with homeschoolers, they have a narrow perspective on their responsibilities as believers. Their families or churches are perceived as the sole context for their Christian responsibilities. Such homeschoolers often ignore the life of their communities.

Churches can sometimes lessen this cultural short-sightedness, except that many churches attracting large numbers of homeschoolers suffer from this same myopic vision of Christian responsibility. Throughout the New Testament, God's people are viewed as a kingdom community that invades and overcomes unbelief instead of retreating and hiding from unbelief. The New Jerusalem is a Holy City—which is to say, a redeemed community and culture rooted in a divine kingdom—not just a family or local church.

The Impact of Covenantal Christian Schooling

All Christian education has its strengths and difficulties. Covenantal Christian schools—that is, schools that admit only students who come from Christian homes—can have a massive and positive impact for Jesus Christ. Let's be honest: At the root of the problems of our culture today is not political liberalism, pollution, public education, or pornography; our present situation is rooted in the fact that bad things happened and God's people did nothing. In a few generations, we have burned through the cultural capital of two millennia. Christian educators are working to rebuild this cultural capital, and I praise the efforts not only of open-admission Christian schools but also covenantal schools.

Still, I maintain that open-admission Christian schooling has greater potential impact than covenantal schooling. The covenantal policy of admitting only students from Christian homes can be based on a desire to prevent the school from having to deal with persons outside the community of faith. Administrators and parents worry that an open-admission policy would lead to compromise, division, and ungodly influences on their Christian students.

A cursory examination of recent history makes their cases seem quite plausible at first. A survey of the last three centuries in the United States would force us to admit, for example, that Harvard University moved from a staunchly Puritan school to a Unitarian school in a matter of years as they admitted persons from a variety of religious backgrounds. Might the same shift away from doctrinal and moral integrity occur in open-admission elementary and secondary schools?

Driven by a desire for theological and ethical purity, many Christian schools limit admissions to students from Christian families. Casual observation suggests, for example, that many schools in the Association of Classical and Christian Schools (ACCS) have some sort of covenantal expectations. Their motives are praiseworthy, and God is doing a great work in many of these schools. Yet I contend that open-admission schools have greater possible potential for positively impacting the world.

What are the problems with covenantal Christian schooling? In the first place, covenantal schools can blur the line between school and church as they make decisions about the souls of families that schools are not qualified to make. Covenantal schools have two options: They can simply require church membership and allow churches to take their proper role in making these decisions, or they can make their own judgments.

In the second option, the schools end up making decisions about Christian discipline and authentic faith that Scripture seems to consign to the local church. There are problems with the first option too: Simply accepting a family's church membership does not mean that any covenant is being upheld. In the confused contemporary tangle of denominational knots and liberalizing equivocations, church membership does not mean the same thing for everyone. Even more problematic, many contemporary churches do not maintain membership rolls, or they practice the ordinances loosely and make no binding judgments about families. This can place the school in any number of potential conflicts with families and with churches.

Like some versions of homeschooling, covenantal Christian education can be driven by a mentality of retreat. Such education looks back at the past two centuries of secularization instead of the past two millennia of Christian history. As a result, some Christians despair and begin to "circle the wagons." Yet this mentality can never lead to triumph. Such a lack of external focus sends powerful signals to the community that this school is not prepared to persuade unbelievers in a loving way. Schools of this stripe seem to look at the community—at unbelievers and perhaps even at believers outside their own faith tradition—as dangerous.

I am more than ready to accept that admitting a student from a non-believing family can also be dangerous. At the same time, I maintain that covenantal Christian schools have not consistently been the strongest harbingers of cultural impact or the maintainers of fruitful faithfulness. At the very least, covenantal Christian schools, with all of their strictures, have performed no better than open-admission schools.

Now back to the examples of early American universities. Would tighter admissions standards, ones admitting only students from strongly Christian families, have maintained the integrity of these schools? No. These fortresses were not victims of hostile takeovers by atheists but rather were compromised internally by people who possessed every membership credential that might be expected to prove they belonged. These tighter standards allowed the most dangerous people to slip through— students and even instructors from Christian families, with well-established membership in churches, but whose faith was heretical or hypocritical.

The decision about which students to admit is more complicated than most covenantal Christian schools want to recognize. Some who could pass through the covenantal filter ought to be rejected. Many students who would never make it through this filter should be admitted because, though they may not even be believers, their willingness to maintain the school's standards may enable God to use the school as a means to make an eternal impact on their lives.

Open-Admission Christian Schools and the Reclamation of Culture

Even non-believers are scrambling out of the darkness of contemporary schooling options. This stream of people, abandoning a failing public education system, will continue to grow. In fact, the question is not whether this stream *will* grow but what our attitude will be when the flood of people reaches our schools. It is easier, of course, to barricade the door and to keep them at bay. Such a response is, however, neither necessary nor helpful.

Christian education must be guarded. Yet, for prospective families who have turned the three keys that I mentioned earlier, the school is taking a risk that is in everyone's best interests. Some believers might balk at allowing non-believers to experience Christian community before committing themselves to the Lord. Yet the school's admissions policy can foster attitudes in students and families of careful, discerning, and purposeful openness.

Christian schools must consider the fact that they are building the schools that could replace the public schools in our land. Such hope of victory and success will no doubt meet with skepticism among people who have seen God's people in retreat for generations. Yet, as I consider the present disintegration of public schools, I am hard-pressed to see any other outcome.

This willingness to take on the responsibility for educating the children of our culture represents a critical step toward reclaiming cultural authority. While we must never forget that charity begins in the household of faith, it cannot end there. This strategy for cultural change bears none of the marks of those grasping paths that Christians have followed in decades past, paths that have rightly led our culture to mock and deride us. It does, however, bear the marks of Jesus' example of the One who "became flesh and pitched His tent among us" (John 1:14, translation mine), and who, while we were yet sinners, loved us and died for us (Rom 5:8). Open-admission Christian schools are poised to make precisely this sort of impact.

I will further contend that classical Christian schools are uniquely poised to make the greatest possible impact on our culture. How? Classical schools are simultaneously building on a strong educational past and moving toward a glorious vision of renewed educational excellence in Western culture. Classical Christian schools are producing excellent students and achieving extraordinary test scores. Perhaps most important, these schools are not hiding from their culture.

At the classical school where I am privileged to serve, high school seniors typically read Frederick Nietzsche's *Beyond Good and Evil* as well as *The Stranger,* by Albert Camus. These are some of the wickedest works ever concocted in any culture. Public schools are wise to keep them off their reading lists. Why then would I require a high school student to read this sort of book? It is because I know that these ideas are already running loose in our culture. Our graduates will be struck with these philosophies when they walk out the doors of our school, and I am preparing them for battle—not of bullets and swords but of false ideologies.

As schools serve families, as children learn truth, and as people flee the present crumbling educational structures in search of goodness and beauty, may they find schools that are vigilant to guard the interests of students and families. May they find schools committed to preserving a Christian environment. May they find schools willing to welcome those who long for their children to be disciplined toward truth, even if these parents and children do not yet know that truth is ultimately found in Jesus.

Open-Admission Christian Schools, the Pathway into the Future

The movement toward open-admission Christian schooling is occurring all over the globe. Do you remember Mr. Stoltzfus? He was the parent headed to an area near one of the most exciting Christian schools in the world. He did indeed deliver our package to that school. And where is that school located?

Kurdistan.

Today, in the Kurdish regions of Iraq, Christian schools are growing. The Kurds—like other tribes in Iraq—are Muslim. Yet this school is far from the typical *madrasah.* It is a classical, open-admission Christian school known as the School of the Medes.[9]

This school has three campuses and serves more than one thousand students. Many of these students are the children of

---

9. For more information, see http://csmedes.org/index.html.

local Iraqi government officials. Ninety-five percent of these students come from Kurdish Muslim families.

Thinking about such a school is sheer joy for me. I know that not all of these students will become Christians, but some of them probably will. Very few, if any, students on these campuses are likely to fight on the side of anti-Western terrorist organizations. The School of the Medes provides a classical Christian education with the consent of Muslim parents and, shockingly, with the support of the local Islamic government! For them, Christian education means excellence in education for both Christians and non-Christians.

What if Christian education in the United States came to mean excellence in education for both Christians and non-Christians? I believe it can. I further believe that this renaissance can begin in small, local Christian schools.

In this difficult time of failed educational expectations, I continually return in my own mind to the thought—to the dream—of seeing small Christian schools throughout the United States renewed so that these schools serve the needs and interests of their communities. One such Christian school might be more convincing and more encouraging in its community than all the government educational programs of the past fifty years. It would bind us to our past and to the proper motive of love. Yet, to be authentic, this would have to be a renaissance accomplished within and for the community itself. It would have to be accomplished, not from the outside by the instruction of visiting experts, but from within as the school pursues ancient principles of neighborly community.[10]

---

10. Language alludes to W. Berry, "The Work of Local Culture," in *What Are People For* (New York: Farrar, 1990).

CHAPTER 4

What Are the Problems with Open-Admission Christian Schooling?

Response by Troy Temple
Perspective of Public Schooling

Many parents considering the private Christian school option will find open-admission Christian schools an attractive choice. The open-admission Christian school has, at the heart, a desire to impact not only Christian families but also the larger culture. If we believe, as Ty asserts, that "poor educational practices have an impact that is far more devastating than any intergalactic calamity that has ever been depicted on the silver screen," we cannot restrict our efforts to Christian families.

Still, I find the open-admission Christian school to represent a questionable methodology, especially when it comes to the potential for evangelism. G. Tyler Fischer suggests that students from every background are potentially eligible for admission in his school. Yet he also admits that students are to be admitted selectively, weeding out potentially problematic students. Ultimately, if the vision of the open-admission Christian school is to admit non-Christian students with the hopes to see them come to know Christ, shouldn't the admissions criteria be structured in such a way as to communicate a strong hope and confidence in God rather than the rejection of "a dangerously reckless teenager"? Does God call us to value the dynamic of "Christian leadership" above the opportunity to share Christ with the troubled teenager?

According to Fischer's chapter, even non-believing students are "expected to talk like believers in Jesus Christ, to submit to authority like believers, to work like believers, and to ask for forgiveness like believers." In this respect, the posture of the open-admission Christian school is most decidedly elitist and demeaning to a non-Christian family. It conveys a disposition that their children are "bad." Furthermore, the expectation that students might need to ramp up academically through extra tutoring as a demonstration of commitment is an extreme hindrance to a missional endeavor. This concept only adds more barriers to the missional intentions.

I would also contend that Ty's use of George Barna's findings as a criticism of public schooling may be out-of-context and misleading. What Ty does not make clear is that, among the 96 percent who do not completely follow their parent's faith, there are children from every schooling option, not public schools alone! The fault is not with public schooling, but with parents who fail to disciple their children adequately.

Response by Mark Eckel
Perspective of Covenantal Christian Schooling

It would be an honor to work in this author's open-admission school. His philosophical point of view shares much in common with my own. We both believe in critical engagement with pagan thinking from a Christian point of view, and teaching young people to practice the craft of Christian apologetics (defense of Christian doctrine) is a major consideration in choosing a Christian school.

I must, however, voice three concerns about open-admission schools: First, some schools are moving toward open-admission out of financial pressure, not because of their mission. Second, the potential loss of distinctiveness in a Christian school may be greater when partnering with unbelieving parents. And third, a focus on training Christian young people may be diminished by the incorporation of evangelistic directives.

If schools are driven by "the bottom line" rather than a Christ-centered mission, pragmatism is the real problem, not open-admission Christian schooling. It is the partnership with unbelievers that may cause the most harm to open-admission schools in the long run. Strong boards and administration notwithstanding, wedding oneself with persons whose views differ radically from one's own may cause difficulties that cannot be foreseen now or repaired in the future.

Still, it is the third concern noted above on which I will focus, that the training of young people is diminished by the incorporation of apologetic and evangelistic directives. Christian faith-learning integration can still occur in open-admission academies. Yet, the time given to an evangelistic-apologetics emphasis could limit the impact of distinctive Christian instruction. What I mean by "evangelistic-apologetics emphasis" is the necessary union of a Christian message for Christian students with the confrontation and refutation of non-Christian ideas brought to class by unbelieving students.

For instance, could an open-admission school teacher honestly say to a class where believers and unbelievers are present, "Every vocation is open to you! Use your God-given passions to engage the whole world"? Can open-admission teachers adequately answer the question, "How does our discipline give praise to God?" when it is possible that not everyone in the class believes in God? Most teachers who are trained by traditional schools of education receive much training in pedagogy, some training in content, but little interdisciplinary preparation. Few institutions train Christian schoolteachers to also serve as evangelists and apologists.

While open-admission schools are clearly committed to Christian cultural engagement, are the teachers in those schools prepared to be evangelistic apologists, weaving their firm biblical beliefs with teaching addressing the needs of unbelieving students? One would hope so.

Response by Michael S. Wilder
Perspective of Homeschooling

Ty Fischer is very passionate about the model of schooling he advocates. Even though I do not fully agree with all of his assumptions about other models, I give him credit for processing the strengths and weaknesses of each.

Let me begin by noting some of our areas of agreement. These areas of agreement include the concept of education *in loco parentis*, the need for parental consideration of education content, a concern for cultural impact, and the recognition that all education is theological. As for the notion of *in loco parentis*, I fully agree that parents are the ones responsible for their children's education. It is the parents' responsibility to decide the *who*, *what*, *how*, and *where* of education. Ty argues, however, that the parent ought to exercise his or her authority by delegating the primary teaching role to educational specialists outside of the home. He rightly quotes the *Shema* in defense of God-centered education with the full knowledge that—at least in the first century AD, perhaps earlier—many Hebrews used synagogue schools to educate their children. Nevertheless, I would not agree with Ty that the first and optimal choice is necessarily to educate children outside the home. I contend that parents are to be the primary disciplers in their children's lives and that schooling is part of the overall process of life-discipleship.

I agree that curricular content must reflect a biblical foundation of absolute truth. It must prepare students to examine the world of senses and the world of ideas within a thoroughly Christian framework. As Ty poignantly notes, "no school—public or religious—is ultimately 'irreligious.' Why? *Because education is an unavoidably theological endeavor.*" This is an argument I have been promoting for years. Every institution, every curriculum, and every teacher possesses certain metaphysical and epistemological beliefs. These beliefs either fit with biblical Christianity or contradict it. There is no middle ground, and that is why Christian parents must pursue Christian education.

I also concur with Ty that Christians must consider their cultural impact. He contends that open-admission Christian schools are the best way to reclaim the present generation and positively impact the future of the American culture. He suggests that this might be accomplished by creating classrooms that consist of fifteen or so believers and a small number of unbelieving students, taught in a Christian worldview by Christian instructors. I would readily admit that such a practice *could* have a positive impact on unbelieving students. Yet to claim that open-admission schools can eventually have the breadth of influence that Ty espouses is fanciful. Apart from educational vouchers, very few American families will ever be able to afford the form of private education that he promotes. For example, a family with household income of $50,000 per year and three children would spend $15,819 per year in a classical Christian school like Veritas Academy—that's 31.6 percent of the family's gross household income![1] This is far beyond the reach of the typical American family. Even if this *were* possible, and even if Christian and non-Christian families throughout North America *did* begin to pursue this sort of education, it would eventually result in an unbalanced classroom ratio between unbelievers and believers—which would impinge on the author's own cardinal rule that Christian influences should outweigh non-Christian influences.

Before concluding this response, I must note a couple of comments made in the open-admission Christian schooling chapter that did elevate my blood pressure a bit. Ty suggests that homeschooling is "often motivated by retreat rather than vision. . . . The greatest impact becomes possible when parents are running towards a vision, not away from a villain." Though environmental and ideological factors are significant factors in the decision-making process for most homeschooling families, I reject the implication that a decision to school at home might represent a decision to huddle in a bunker without concern for a lost world. And to suggest that large numbers of homeschooling families operate without a definite vision is unreasonable. I contend that the primary rationale for Christian homeschooling is a clear vision of raising up a godly generation of individuals who

---

1. http://www.veritasacademy.com/index.php?option=com_content&task=view&id=12&Itemid=13

are well-equipped with a biblical worldview and well-prepared to fulfill God's cultural mandate to obey the Great Commission.

The second comment that concerns me relates to the long-term impact of homeschooling. Ty proposes that once home-schooled children graduate, any positive impact that can occur directly through the practice of home education is finished. In fact, the positive impact will continue from generation to generation as they train their own children in a biblical worldview and prepare them to fulfill the Great Commission.

Counter-Response by G. Tyler Fischer
Perspective of Open-Admission Christian Schooling

Having read my fellow contributors' responses, I want to thank them for their criticisms. They did a great job of seeing some of the practical and philosophical weaknesses in my argument and they were kind in their critiques. I will respond here to a few of the more pertinent criticisms.

Speaking for the perspective of public schooling, Troy Temple declares that open-admission schools play both sides of the admissions issue, claiming to be open to all people while at the same time weeding out potentially problematic students. This is a valid criticism. I have a limited number of desks and teachers. Within these limitations, I must choose the students that best fit our mission and vision. When I have more seats, I will continue to do this but I will be able to accept more students. I will work to maintain the same standards—teaching students to love Christ, to love learning, and to develop environments that can reflect Christ's truth, beauty, and goodness. If a student refuses to conform to these standards, I will kick the student out—whether he professes Christ or not!

One should note, however, the deeper problem behind Troy's criticism. It is that the criticism exposes the horrific weakness of public schools. Public schools have practically *no* limitations on admission, and increasingly no objective standards for discipline or truth. Would it be too much to say having "no limits" eventually leads to having "no standards"? I think not. Until the public schools throw off a philosophy that proclaims a radically standardless world, a world where the education of a child can supposedly happen without reference to Jesus Christ as the focal point of all wisdom and knowledge, folly will result. In fact, it already has. Some limits are necessary for authentic, excellent, truth-centered education to occur.

Mark Eckel, speaking from the perspective of covenantal Christian schooling, criticizes my position from the opposite perspective. Mark asks if open-admission teachers adequately answer the question "How does our discipline give praise to God?" when it is possible that not everyone in the class believes in God. Basically, Mark is asking how an open-admission school can emphasize Christ if some of the students may not be believers. My response is that we can and we do. We do so because every student bears God's image and every student is called by the gospel to repent of his sins, to turn to Christ, and to follow Him. We possess no power to change a student's heart; only the Holy Spirit can do that. We can, however, teach transcendent truth and enforce standards for behavior that are rooted in the character and nature of God.

My final answer to Mark's critique, however, is simply this: Requiring all students and families to profess Christ does not mean that covenantal Christian schools somehow get a pass on this problem! After all, some people who say they have experienced the work of the Holy Spirit have not—or at least they act as if they have not. We call our students (and I am confident that Mark would do the same) to follow Christ today, to repent today, to believe the gospel today, and to love their neighbors today. All Christian education must do this.

Finally, Michael Wilder raises a great practical objection from the perspective of home education asking how it is even possible for people to afford open-admission classical Christian schooling. As Michael points out, "a family with household income of $50,000 per year and three children would spend $15,819 per year in a classical Christian school like Veritas Academy—that's 31.6 percent of the family's gross household income!"

Ouch! The sting of practicality! Who let *him* on *our* Web site? This is a very valid concern, and it changes the field substantially. But I suggest the question really should not be "How can I afford this?" The appropriate question is, "Is it worth it?" My best answer to that is simply, "Come and see." Of those who do come and see, many say it definitely is worth it. Some, like me, even think it is a bargain.

There are other reasons to hope that people can afford to attend our school: First, the money exists. As we speak, it costs roughly $42,000 per child to educate those same children in the public school system where Veritas Academy resides. (See what a bargain we are!) The public education system is collapsing. Eventually, as public schooling systems continue to crumble, there could well be more money made available to educate children in open-admission Christian schools.

Additionally, this price tag has to be balanced against the price tag of *not* paying tuition, as in Michael's case of homeschooling. The costs of home education are less visible, but they are real. If a homeschooling mother teaches her three children forty hours each week for forty weeks each year, she is working at a rate of $9.38 an hour to recoup the $15,819 that she could be paying to Veritas Academy for her children's tuition. The reality, however, is that some moms work a lot more than this. How much absence of Mom from other places is acceptable? When does the Proverbs 31 woman decide that making garments and buying vineyards is better for her family than trying to teach chemistry, *The Divine Comedy,* and advanced calculus? Whose economics are unreasonable? Each family must make its own call on this point, based on what God leads them to do, but that point does exist. Too many people pass over it.

Thanks to the editor and to my esteemed fellow writers! I have enjoyed this endeavor and hope that we can continue this discussion at some point, if not now then in glory.

CHAPTER 5

Christian Schools for Christian Families
HOW COVENANTAL SCHOOLS PARTNER WITH CHRISTIAN PARENTS TO CO-TRAIN STUDENTS FOR LIFE

By Mark Eckel

K. C., given a full-ride doctoral scholarship to the University of Chicago in art history, said, "God has called me to live, study, and work in a secular academic environment. Because of my Christian school experience, I've been able to maintain my faith, to grow in Christ, and to challenge the perspectives of those around me. I was taught how to be 'in the world but not of it.'"

Steve came to the seventh-grade interview for new students. He was quiet but honest in his answers. When asked why he wanted to attend our Christian school, he replied, "I want to find God here." Steve went on to become one of my student chaplains.

Corien declared that Christian schooling had equipped her son to analyze and to evaluate the world around him. "Taylor has been equipped to discern the world in which he will live because he was taught to look at life through the guidelines given in Scripture."

These are just a few examples of how covenantal Christian education contributes to lasting life-change. So what is a covenantal Christian school? A "covenant" is, of course, an arrangement between two parties for a common purpose. In this chapter, I will be using the term "covenantal" to describe a Christian school that only admits students from Christian households. In covenantal education, Christian schools and Christian parents come together to co-train the next generation of believers. As you consider where and how to educate your child, I ask you to consider the possibility that a covenantal Christian school may provide the best possible context for your child's education.

Although the term "covenantal Christian schooling" may have its deficiencies, other descriptors of this sort of schooling introduce more confusion than clarity. Detractors occasionally refer to covenantal education as "closed-admission Christian schooling," usually in contrast to "open-admission Christian schooling." It is true that admission to a covenantal school *is* closed to non-Christian families. Yet "closed-admission" places the emphasis on who is *excluded* instead of emphasizing how covenantal schools positively partner with a broad range of Christian families.

Other researchers have referred to covenantal schools as "discipleship-oriented schools."[1] While this terminology captures part of the purpose of covenantal education, "discipleship-oriented" may give the impression that covenantal schools primarily focus on developing a vibrant spiritual life in students. Covenantal educational *can* cultivate spiritual disciplines in students; however, a well-conceived covenantal Christian school is far more comprehensive, partnering with parents to train students to think Christianly in *every* area of life and academics. Given the deficiencies of other available terminologies, "covenantal Christian education" remains the best available descriptor of schooling that enrolls only children from Christian households and trains them in a Christian curriculum.

---

1. See, e.g., T. Kaiser, forthcoming doctoral dissertation (Louisville, Ky.: The Southern Baptist Theological Seminary, 2010).

Why Covenantal Christian Schooling?

What should compel Christian parents to spend extra time, money, and effort to send their son or daughter to a covenantal Christian school? To be honest, some families commit to Christian education, whether covenantal or open-admission, for all the wrong reasons. Some dads and moms send their offspring to Christian schools simply because they can. Prestige, status, or a consumer approach to educational options contribute to these parents' decision.[2] Other parents may believe that Christian schools offer better discipline, safer environments, or better opportunities for higher education.

Perhaps most parents enroll their children in Christian schools for far more lofty reasons. They sincerely desire to build a Christian worldview in their children from the inside out. I am convinced that covenantal Christian schools are the best places to build this sort of worldview. A well-conceived covenantal education builds a Christian worldview in your child through biblical structure, stature, posture, exposure, and nurture for school-age children.

Biblical Structure. Covenantal schools consciously partner with Christian parents and students to provide a biblical framework that builds God-centered purpose into every part of life. Rooted in the Bible, school mission statements should be fleshed out in the continual classroom intersection of supernatural and natural worlds. Teachers must be hired and trained first and foremost for their commitment to training children from a Christian perspective, lesson in and lesson out. Administration and board should practice the shepherding of their staff, protecting and providing for their educational needs.

Stature. People want schools to take a stand, to hold a position, to stake their reputation on a mission. Committed Christian parents understand that a culture committed to materialism must be confronted with trained young people committed to the Lord of the material world. In schools that take their stature seri-

---

2. M. Eckel, "Selling the School: A Christian Response to the Consumer Education Model," *Christian Educator's Journal*, 2004.

ously, community standing is enhanced not primarily by external recognition, but by lives lived in service to others.

Posture. Documents and declarations are not enough. A Christian school's reputation should be something enacted not only through words but also through attitudes and actions, in and before the community. Knowledge seen through the lens of Scripture should produce a posture of humility and love. Parents want to see this Christian mind-set in the lives of teachers, wrapped with passion for the subject and compassion for the student.

Exposure. Christian parents know that the tried and true principles of life have ancient, heavenly origins. They want their students' roots sunk deep in the soil of biblical and theological truth. At the same time, wise parents and schools know that other research and discoveries—often from non-Christian and even anti-Christian sources—may help their children to articulate and defend a biblical worldview. In covenantal schools, formed through partnerships of believing families, ideas from sources outside the Christian faith are analyzed in the context of timeless truth. Joe, a Christian school teacher, stated the reason for Christian schools in this way: "I don't want to give students new tools; I want to give them a brand new toolbox." Joe is the kind of educator the Christian parent seeks. Certain facts about math, science, history, and literature remain the same, regardless of one's educational philosophy. In a covenantal school, however, the distinctively Christian context and curriculum equips students with a different container in which even these truths are viewed in light of biblical truth. Covenantal schools carefully and purposefully expose students to alternative perspectives to train them to articulate and to defend their faith.

Nurture. There is a natural need and desire to shelter tender youngsters as they grow. This shelter must, however, be focused on the goal of preparation for real life. Christian parents need Christian teachers who are masters of content and communication to provide their children with biblical buoys to follow, navigating turbulent cultural seas throughout their lives. Only in a covenantal Christian school can the interior development of a young life be rooted in a commitment, shared by school and home, to Jesus Christ as the Lord of all life. Biblical structure, stature, posture, exposure, and nurture can create a foundation for Christian lives that will impact the culture with Christ's Lordship for the next generation.

What Covenantal Christian Schooling Provides for Your Child

Derek sat in the stuffed chair on the other side of my desk. "Why do we have to learn all those details about theology? I mean, really, why are you so concerned about how words are used?" His tone told me that this was no disrespectful challenge; it was a serious question.

"Are you still going to vocational courses in the afternoon?" I inquired.

"Uh-huh," he nodded. "Auto mechanics."

"Have you ever used a micrometer to take a measurement?"

Derek slid forward in the seat, hands moving to illustrate his point.

"Yeah! See"—now the student began to teach me—"it's really important that the measurement of the pistons is exact. If there's even the slightest variance, you lose precision in the engine and—," he stopped mid-sentence.

A smile slid across his face as he turned toward the door, "I get it, Mr. Eckel. I get it now."

The precision necessary for a car to run well is the same sort of precision that ought to be expected in learning. Exactness in grammar counts. Math problems must be completed correctly. Intricate details are absolute in chemistry. Theology is no different. A person's belief system should function like a fine-tuned engine. Covenantal Christian schooling offers your child an educational experience focused far more precisely than any other educational option. Specifically, covenantal schooling offers *meaning, permanence,* and *a precious heritage.*

Covenantal Christian schooling reveals meaning. At some point in school, everyone has heard the question, usually voiced in a high-pitched whine: "Why do I have to learn *this?*" Children have been raising this query since before the days of Moses. Although the child's attitude may not always be the best, it reveals a universal truth: God created human life and learning to have purpose, reason, and meaning. Having a purpose is what gets a person out of bed in the morning.

The Hebrews knew that the ultimate meaning, purpose, and reason for everything was rooted in the character and identity of God. When children asked what the Passover meant (Exod 12:24–28) or what was the purpose of the law code (Deut 6:20–25), Israelite parents knew that their children were asking theological questions. Educational ceremonies were literally a work, labor, or service—which is to say, these ceremonies had a goal and a purpose.[3]

When I taught high school students I began each semester by discussing biblical reasons why a Christian school exists. Here is a snippet of what I told them. Among the Israelites, the meaningfulness of education—the *why* of schooling—was rooted in three specific factors: *time, place,* and *people.* A Christian school should be rooted in these same three factors. A school's greatest impact is directly tied to how much *time* is spent in a certain *place* with the right teachers training *people* to think and live.

When it comes to the three factors time, place, and people, consider the impact of covenantal education. Your child typically will spend seven hours a day, 180 days a year in school. That equals 1,260 hours in school each year, not counting activities before and after school. It is not just how much time young people spend that makes education meaningful, though; it is also where and with whom they spend it. When it comes to the meaningfulness of the time, the place, and the people, doesn't it seem wisest to place your child in a context where Christian teachers actively partner with Christian parents to train children in a biblical worldview?

Covenantal Christian schooling has permanence. A sign hanging in a Christian school weight room reads, "I do not fear failure as much as I fear that I will be successful at things which

---

3. V. Hamilton, *The Book of Genesis: Chapters 1–17* (Grand Rapids, Mich.: Eerdmans, 1990), 142.

really do not matter." The problem with many popular models of education has to do with *the loss of lasting goals*. Often, this results in schools being successful at things that do not ultimately matter.

In many schools, the leadership chases the latest and newest curriculum ideas. Novelties, fads, and trends drive school decisions. The result is that schools pursue temporary values instead of lasting virtues. The difference between values and virtues is crucial: Values do not last; virtues do. Values are based on consumer authority. Virtues are rooted in everlasting truth. Schools that pursue values instead of virtues find themselves influenced by market influences and demographic whims instead of lasting truth. Throughout Scripture, that which matters is said to be everlasting (Pss 102:12; 104:31; 112:3; 117:2; 118:1–4; 119:89; 145:13). Christians are even told to "focus on . . . what is unseen" (2 Cor 4:18). Why? Because the virtues that last are not tangible or corporeal—they are intangible and eternal.

Since lasting virtue is rooted in explicitly religious confessions, public schooling—rooted as it is in secular values—has been denuded of anything that might epitomize permanence. While educators in an open-admission Christian school may aim toward developing permanence, lasting virtue cannot be developed in the school alone. Partnerships with Christian parents—the sort of partnerships that covenantal schools uniquely provide—are crucial to the development of authentic virtue in students.

Here are some questions that could identify permanence in a Christian school: Does the school view students as disciples of an everlasting kingdom or does the school fill seats on some other basis? Does the school highlight athletic success or focus on physical talent for God's glory? Does the school center attention on physical facilities or does the school view its facilities as tools for building community? Does the school first hire faculty based on their commitment to partner with parents or on a cultural need for state certification?

Perhaps Wendell Berry said it best, "A proper education enables young people to put their lives in order, which means knowing what things are more important than other things; it means putting first things first."[4] As covenantal schools practice permanence, students acknowledge the truth behind the words in the weight room: Some things *do* matter more than others.

Covenantal Christian schooling preserves a precious heritage. "You ruined watching movies for me, forever!" the student jokingly chided. That is one of the many unsolicited comments I have received from students in response to my passion for helping them to watch films from a Christian point of view. In the classroom, teachers pass on what they view as important, even if it is something as basic as how to watch a movie. Put another way, every teacher passes on a heritage to his or her students.

The concept of heritage is a crucial theme throughout the Hebrew Scriptures. From the perspective of the Hebrews, since the earth belonged to God (Deut 10:14), only God could give land as a permanent possession (1 Kgs 8:36). That is why moving a boundary marker represented such a significant lapse in covenantal faithfulness (Deut 19:14; 27:17; Prov 23:10). In Israel, property was preserved for succeeding generations and was never to be forfeited (Lev 25:23,28; cf. 1 Kgs 21:3–4). What was passed on was based on a permanent right, given by God's grace; it was a person's *heritage.*

From a biblical perspective, there is much that every Christian is responsible to preserve as a heritage. God Himself is our heritage (Ps 119:57; 142:5); the laws of the Creator are our legacy (Ps 119:111); children are our cherished inheritance (Ps 127:3). As Christians in the Western world, we have another heritage to preserve and to protect. This heritage is not made up of soil or stone, however. It is an ancient conversation of imagination and ideas rooted in the Judeo-Christian foundations of Western society. Os Guinness put it this way with reference to classic literature:

> With endless controversies swirling around the Western masterworks, individual followers of Christ and the church of Christ as a whole have a unique responsibility to guard, enjoy, and pass them on. Christians should stand alongside

---

4. W. Berry, "Thoughts in the Presence of Fear," in *The Presence of Fear: Three Essays for a Changed World* (Great Barrington, Mass.: Orion, 2001), 9.

people of many faiths and allegiances who treasure the priceless heritage of this three-thousand-years' conversation of imagination and ideas—not least because they are privileged to share the faith that animated the majority of these masterworks.[5]

A covenantal Christian school—rooted in partnership between Christian parents and Christian school—represents the prime context for the preservation of this precious and multifaceted heritage.

How Does the Covenantal Christian School Work?

One mother said to me, "*Why* the school exists is shown by *how* the school functions. My child is encouraged to produce creation pictures in art. She discusses Christian principles in science. And she interacts with the impact of the Creator's principles in history." That's precisely how covenantal education ought to operate.

The *why* and the *how* are inseparable in covenantal education. To illustrate the foundations of *why* these schools exist as well as *how* they function as a result, let us look at the pyramid illustration included in this chapter, beginning with *philosophy*.

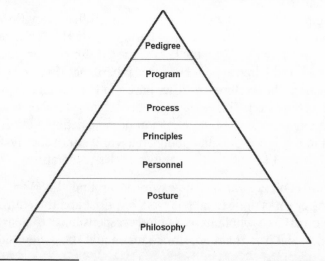

---

5. O. Guinness and L. Cowan, eds., *Invitation to the Classics* (Grand Rapids, Mich.: Baker, 1998), 14.

Philosophy. A school's philosophy includes a *mission* that defines its identity, a *vision* that tells where it is headed, and *core virtues* that explain how it plans to get there based on biblical truths. For a school's philosophy to function well, parents and teachers must share passion for the same truth.

For many decades, the English occupied Ireland. Teaching Irish tradition or culture was forbidden. Irish parents employed *hedgemasters* to instruct their children. These instructors taught in out-of-the-way spots, like hedgerows, caves, or isolated fields. Avoiding English authority, the hedgemasters continued their instruction despite threats of imprisonment, even death. They taught with passion because their heritage depended on it.

Covenantal schoolteachers operate like Irish hedgemasters because they partner with parents to train children, and they teach knowing that the survival of a precious heritage depends on their teaching. Partnered with Christian parents, covenantal Christian educators teach the traditional subject areas from a decidedly Christian point of view. In geography, for example, students might learn that God established the times and places of all people (Gen 10; Acts 17:24–28). In Spanish, French, or German classes, the teacher might show how many dialects descended from one shared source, suggesting a common human origin (Acts 17:26; 1 Cor 15:44–49; Eph 3:14–15). Loving one's neighbor (Mark 12:30–31) is key in a Christian sociology class. The emphasis on unity that fills Paul's epistle to the Ephesians (2:14–18; 3:14–15; 4:1–6) should help to break down misunderstandings, stereotypes, and prejudices. Science and math classes demonstrate how everything was organized and arranged in what we call a "cosmos"—an orderly world (see Gen 2:1).[6] A Christian view of everything—a philosophy centered in Jesus as the originator and sustainer of all wisdom (Col 2:3)—thrives in a covenantal context where teachers and parents share a common goal of passing on a Christian heritage.

---

6. The function of *sebaot* suggests that God brought together all different parts of creation into an orderly collection. J. Hartley, *sebaot*, in *The Theological Wordbook of the Old Testament*, ed. R. Harris, G. Archer, and B. Waltke (Chicago, Ill.: Moody, 1980), 2:750.

Posture. The posture of a covenantal school entails commitment to certain habits of the heart. These habits include Christian intellect, interiority,[7] and involvement in the community in ways that intersect and infuse the life of the school. Here is how one covenantal school described its posture: "Alexis de Tocqueville, the French sociologist, visited America at the beginning of the nineteenth century to see what made the country distinctive. [He] discovered a population which lived life based on unwavering, religious principles. He referred to these internal barometers as 'habits of the heart.' At Trinity Christian School we believe 'habits of the heart' should build children from the inside, out." Only co-committed Christian families and teachers can weave a philosophy that enables such a posture.

An example of how the posture of a covenantal school differs from other options is that extrinsic rewards are considered to be natural parts of the educational process in most institutions. These extrinsic rules of conformity train children to seek immediate gratification and rewards. Yet the most desirable changes—the ones that are truly lasting and worthwhile—are internal and intangible. Love and freedom (Prov 11:21; 14:22) represent intangible yet real effects of righteous living, not of seeking extrinsic motivations (see Prov 10:6,24; 13:21,25; 29:18).

In a covenantal school, correct posture might include a third-grade teacher's classroom goals. Instead of pursuing extrinsic rewards and conformity, she might say, "Believing every child is a whole person, created by God in His image, yet corrupted by sin, we will seek to sustain a climate of grace so that every word and action mirrors God's generous gift to us (Eph 2:8–10; 4:32), to establish gentle measures of correction for every wayward attitude since we have been afforded many 'second chances' (Prov 28:13–14), to encourage the creative endowments of children recognizing that everyone is gifted by God and created in His image (Gen 1:28; 2:15; Exod 31:1–5), and to identify the routine goodness of God in every aspect of life (Ps 107; Eccl 5:18–20)."

---

7. "Interiority" can best be defined as having died to self as our "life is now hidden with the Messiah in God" (Col 3:3). Renunciation and relinquishment of everything that would impede the process of growth in Christ develops the inward life of the Christian. See J. Houston, *Joyful Exiles* (Downers Grove, Ill.: InterVarsity, 2006), 31–50.

Lasting habits of the heart develop over time in young lives as Christian parents and Christian teachers practice truth in their dealings with children.

Personnel. Christian teachers *are* the school. God-gifted teachers demonstrate the school's philosophy and live the school's posture. Scripture is clear about the kind of people with whom we should educationally align ourselves. Board members, administrators, staff, and faculty should ascribe to 2 Timothy 1:14: "Guard, through the Holy Spirit who lives in us, that good thing entrusted to you." Degrees and certifications, while important in some cases, cannot turn a teacher into "living curriculum" (2 Cor 3:2). Spurring one another on to "love and good works" is fully possible only within the covenantal context of a shared "confession of our hope" in Christ that binds teachers and parents together (Heb 10:23–24).

Principles. Christian parents who want their children exposed to a Christian interpretation of life that unifies all studies should choose covenantal Christian schooling. The underlying principles of covenantal education are that all of life is unified and that all of life belongs to God. Examples in the classroom would include recognitions that classification in any discipline is based on Adam's "naming," following a pattern set by God (Gen 1:5,8,10; 2:19–20,23); that we should value reading because, through reading, we can encounter the Word of God (Ps 141:2; 142:2); that legitimate authority derives from God and not from human efforts to gain power (Prov 28:15; 29:2,4,7,12,14,16); and that even hygiene and sanitation are divinely-ordained for human benefit (Exod 29:14; Lev 12:1–4; Deut 23:12–14).

One elementary teacher put it this way: "The five senses cannot be taught Christianly unless there is a sixth sense, a sense of Someone who has given us our senses." An instructor in physical education said, "I tell my classes when they hurt themselves, pain is God's gift so that we discontinue the exercise to stop further injury." The covenantal school partners with Christian parents to point children constantly to God's universe, saying, Look! See! In the covenantal school, studying everything from airplane wings to classic literature, from biological phyla to personal hygiene, depends on harmonizing biblical principles with daily life in home and at school.

Process. Principles must be enacted through a process. This process allows for the communication of biblically-integrated thinking throughout the school and in the community. *Integrating biblical truth for life.* This motto was plastered everywhere: engraved on business cards, etched in plaques in the hallway, painted on the sides of buses. It was the motto I suggested in a school where I was privileged to teach for a decade. "Integrating biblical truth for life" was taught, discussed, and practiced by the faculty every day. Mission and vision statements reflected this point of view. The phrase was expounded at public events, reiterated at parent-teacher conferences, and publicized in the community. Teachers from the school were asked to speak in their areas of expertise at conventions and colleges because they had become experts in biblical integration.

Imagine a Christian school where biblical truths so permeated the day that one hears morning announcements like this one: "Genesis 1:28 states that humans bear responsibility to 'rule' the earth. As students, learning more about the world around us is our God-given responsibility. It is part of what we do to 'rule' the world. May the Creator who has given us thinking minds be pleased with our efforts this day as we seek to obey His command by bringing our studies under His authority."

Or consider the possibility of this parent-teacher memo anywhere but in a covenantal Christian context: "In 1 Chronicles 29:11, it is written that everything in heaven and earth belongs to God. If God has been pleased to place us here as His servants in acquiring knowledge, we must do two things: (1) Acknowledge that every part of life—including our time in school—is owned by God, and (2) find pleasure in the task of displaying God's ownership of life through our studies."

As a parent, do you desire a school that articulates a Christian perspective during study-time, lunch, recess, and athletic events? If so, a covenantal Christian school is the best choice. Seeking fully integrated growth in the wisdom of Christ in every part of life (Eph 1:17; Phil 1:9–10; Col 1:9) requires a co-curricular, cooperative, coherent Christian mind-set. In a well-conceived covenantal school, "integrating biblical truth for life" is not simply a school motto; it is what school personnel eat, sleep, and breathe.

Program. Another term for *program* would be *curriculum.* In a covenantal Christian school, the curriculum must be distinct. I spoke with a newly-named superintendent who recognized this truth. She was intent on changing her Christian school's culture, and she said to me before a seminar: "If you compare our class and course descriptions with those of other schools in the area, you would see no difference at all." The look on her face spoke volumes about her commitment to change this circumstance. Another Christian headmaster put the point bluntly: "If my school's Advanced Placement Calculus course is no different from the public school down the street, I tell people, 'Go there! It's free!'"

Biblical truths sustain every aspect of the school day in a covenantal school. Classroom philosophies find their origin in Scripture. Classroom goals are heaven's Word maintained in the school's work. Units of study are framed by biblical objectives. Lesson plans clearly point to the interconnections of the supernatural and natural worlds.

The Christian math teacher should know, for instance, that because sin has disrupted God's world, "showing one's work" is essential to maintain accuracy. In English, corrections finished for a paper's second draft show human limitations; fallen and finite people need repetition and correction. Second-graders might be instructed by their teacher that God's pattern of hard work followed by rest is analogous to studying hard before recess. The art teacher is convinced from the Bible that beauty and usefulness go together (see Gen 2:9). Christian parents are best served when their children experience such Christian curriculum in a Christian context.

Pedigree. The capstone of the pyramid is *pedigree.* I would summarize the pedigree of a covenantal school by saying *children are indoctrinated Christianly to transform culture through their vocational lives.* The word *pedigree* is chosen carefully to suggest a pure bloodline. Christians are to be different from beginning to end. Christian teachers are called to train "the next genera-tion" (see Ps 71:14–18; Acts 13:36) to be committed in such a way that they live as aliens and strangers in the land (Lev 19:34; 1 Pet 2:11). Of course, some forms of indoctrination are illegitimate. Yet, in truth, every school indoctrinates—notice *doctrine* in the root of this word—by communicating certain worldviews.

Students ten, twenty, twenty-five years removed from the classroom testify to vocational commitments that have been woven into their lives through covenantal Christian education. Kate and I discussed treatment of mental illness as we ate break-fast together. "Medical institutions often overmedicate patients to keep them . . . well, almost in a trance," Kate began. She is a nurse in a psychiatric ward. "They're easier to handle that way, we are told. But as a Christian, I can't remain silent when doc-tors and nurses discuss patient care. These patients are made in God's image, and I want us to treat them as whole people. I want us to deal with mental illness better than we do."

Craig and John have described the results of their education in this way: "We were taught to think, and to think as Chris-tians." Both of these men have earned doctorates; they now serve as professors of philosophy and communications, respectively. Craig and John are now applying what they learned from their covenantal education as they teach college students.

Doctors testify that they view patients more holistically be-cause they saw how Scriptural truth intersects with science. Law-yers protect client rights because of what they learned in high school about Old Testament law codes. Other former students, now retailers, tell me how they believe in serving people instead of padding the bottom line. Businessmen, police officers, home-makers, teachers, and publishers trained in covenantal Christian schools invert cultural expectations, creating godly change in their vocations and communities.

How Do Covenantal Christian Educators Answer Critics?

To be fair, there are thoughtful Christian people who believe that communities can be transformed through educational involvement in homeschooling, open-admission Christian school-ing, or public schooling. While I respect these believers, I find each of these positions to be deficient.

Homeschooling? Friends who homeschool their children have asked me, "Can a Christian school really provide our chil-dren with the same personal attention that we give? What if a teacher's convictions differ from ours? How can the covenantal Christian school hope to give the same instruction as a student's parents?"

Both of these homeschooling parents had earned master's degrees—one in the humanities, one in the sciences. Mom stayed home with the children. In the evenings, Dad answered queries about science. Once a week, the children met with other homeschoolers for games and activities.

I was forced to admit, "Your concerns are right, and your instruction is beyond reproach. In fact, I would have to add that many famous leaders have been homeschooled at some point or another—Theodore Roosevelt, Winston Churchill, and C. S. Lewis—and you practice the intention of Deuteronomy chap-ter 6. You reinforce instruction throughout the day."

The homeschooling parents beamed.

"But let's be honest," I launched my review, "most home-schooling parents do not have your educational backgrounds or your support network. In all fairness, a well-established cove-nantal Christian school is the best place to offer a broader view of the Christian faith, a community of discipleship with committed Christian teachers, and collective expertise in subject areas that most folks simply do not have."

I was surprised by their response: "You're right," they said. "Even in our own homeschooling community, we are more the exception than the rule."

Open-Admission Christian Schools? I have also had the honor of interacting with many Christian schools that exist be-cause they want to meet the needs of all people—even those who do not come from Christian homes. Open-admission Christian school leaders have suggested that transforming culture from a Christian point of view is the most advantageous position to take in a pluralistic society. I laud these open-admission school administrators and teachers for their desire to transform culture by training even those who have not trusted Jesus Christ. The opportunities for interacting with divergent ideas in the classroom are exceptional.

These leaders have often said to me that covenantal Christian schools are too narrow in their focus. I admit, some covenantal Christian schools tend toward isolationist perspectives. There are covenantal schools that ascribe so deeply to Americanized nationalism that any authentic interest in other cultures or countries is excluded. Other covenantal academies are rooted so deeply in a particular church or denomination that they fail to appreciate global or historical perspectives on Christianity.

But this does not have to be the case: When I taught in covenantal Christian schools, my students interacted with *The Humanist Manifesto*. They compared and contrasted the Declaration of Independence (American, 1776) with the Declaration of the Rights of Man (French, 1789). They engaged the ideas of Nietzsche, Rousseau, Ralph Waldo Emerson, Edgar Allan Poe, William Golding, Joseph Campbell, and many others. I trained students how to interpret popular music and movies. In our classrooms, local college professors discussed ethics, the existence of God, and whether or not the Bible was simply one myth among many. In their senior year my students wrote a twenty-page "Christian Manifesto" without referring explicitly to Jesus or to Scripture. Before pupils went to college, this Christian Manifesto trained them to construct and to defend transcendent principles for life in a secular context. Covenantal Christian schools can and do consistently engage culture without becoming isolated. When they do not, the fault is not with their model of schooling but with the content of their instruction.

Public Schooling? Knowing I was a Christian school educator, one Christian parent approached me saying, "Christians are abandoning the public square. Having Christians in public education brings salt and light to the community. My child is a consistent witness in her public high school. Everyone knows she's a Christian. People respect her points of view on sex, drugs, alcohol, and creation."

I praised his daughter's stance, acknowledging that she would surely be able to provide alternative perspectives in the classrooms of her public school. Then, I said, "Of course, you spend a couple of hours each night reviewing the teaching that your child has received during the day, don't you?"

The dad looked confused.

"For instance," I became more specific, "you are reading all the books assigned in her literature class, right? And you help your daughter to see each author's intentions from a Christian perspective? In history, you help her to compare the common assumption that 'history repeats itself' with the Christian view that history has a purpose. In math and science, you are concerned about the claims that humans construct systems of thought rather than the view that people simply discover what God has already placed in His creation. Right?"

This father was not taking responsibility for developing a biblical worldview in his daughter. What is worse, he himself did not even see that a Christian worldview is not simply about taking a certain stance on sexual ethics and creation science. A Christian worldview consciously chooses to make sense of life in ways that are fundamentally incompatible with the world's perspective. This father assumed that some areas of study were somehow neutral. But there is no neutrality in education, not in math, literature, history, or anything else. Education is theological, through and through.

What Covenantal Education Provides. A covenantal Christian school provides the prime context for children to learn how to identify, to analyze, and to critique non-biblical perspectives. We do not send people into battle simply because they are on our side, and we recognize that soldiers must be trained to meet the enemy before they reach the battlefield. In the battle for students' minds, Christians should train young people with the tools necessary to combat pagan ideas. Being "salt and light" assumes that the salt has a distinctive Christian flavor and that the light is bright enough to pierce the darkness. Covenantal Christian education trains children to be salt and light before they find themselves enmeshed in battle.

Training for Life from Beginning to End

The word "Deuteronomy" literally means "the second law." God's statutes had to be repeated anew to a generation born in the wilderness (Deut 1:39). Moses told the generation of Israelites that he addressed in Deuteronomy that their future responsibility as parents included training their children (4:5–8; 6:1–9,20–25; 11:1–11). The word that Moses used to describe this training is the same term that was used when someone sharpened a knife on a whetstone. The action had to be continuous, in the same direction (6:7). The word carried the idea both of starting and of completion. One might say that it describes proper training from "beginning to end."[8] With that in mind, let us summarize what covenantal schooling offers, repeating the essence of how covenantal education trains children from beginning to end.

Wholeness. Student life in a Christian school is not to be seen in parts—spiritual, physical, social, emotional, intellectual. The Greek concept dividing "secular" from "sacred" goes against the Hebraic concept of wholeness, completion, fulfillment in *shalom.* Instead of separating aspects of life into pieces, the covenantal school is concerned with the whole child, restoring all things because of Jesus' reconciliation (2 Cor 5:17–20; Col 1:15–20).

Meaning. The answer to "why" provides a foundation for purpose. Over and over God instructed parents to give reasons for the "why" questions (Exod 12:24–28; Deut 6:20–25; Josh 4:1–9,19–24). If there is no meaning, then there is no indicative—no *something* to believe in. And if there is no indicative, there is no imperative—no necessity or urgency that drives us to answer anyone's questions (cf. Prov 22:17–21).

Coherence. How does everything fit together? How does life make sense? There must be an intersection and unification of heaven and earth, supernatural and natural. From the very first

---

8. J. A. Hermann, *shanan,* in *TWOT* 2:943.

statement in Scripture, unity and wholeness were necessary—the "heavens and the earth" meant everything from A to Z in the Hebrew mind-set. From God's very first statement to humans, there is a unity of Truth.

God does not repeat Himself to hear Himself talk. Like the child in school, everyone needs to be reminded of essentials. Parents making choices for their child's education must consider the foundations that will be built within their offspring for a dozen years or more. The Christian school in partnership with Christian families provides the best possible internal framework, shaping whole persons for the whole world for their whole lives.

CHAPTER 6

What Are the Problems with Covenantal Christian Schooling?

Response by Troy Temple
Perspective of Public Schooling

One of our favorite professional sports in the United States is football. On the field, teams approach each series of plays with great intentionality. Before each snap of the ball, before players walk up to the line of scrimmage, they huddle. Only players on the field can be in the huddle. The quarterback calls a play that tells each player what to do to advance the ball. Between the huddle and the snap of the ball, something crucial happens: The players break the huddle. You see, no matter how much talent the team has on the field or how great the play may be, the play will never happen if the players stay in the huddle.

The covenantal Christian school offers a great opportunity for Christian families to have their child's education developed under the influence of teachers who share a similar worldview. Every Christian parent should desire that his or her child learns to see the hand of God in every aspect of creation. But the strength of covenantal Christian schooling is also its greatest weakness. The covenantal schools have become proficient in the huddle and seldom deploy young believers to serve the Great Commission beyond Christian vocational ministries.

As Mark introduced his chapter, he noted three real-life examples to bolster his case for choosing a covenantal Christian school. First, K. C., who received a full scholarship to the University of Chicago, testified that her covenantal Christian school experience equipped her to be "in the world but not of it." While that sentiment echoes the heart of Jesus' ministry in the gospels, it seems somewhat questionable considering the stance of covenantal Christian schools. Covenant schools control enrollment with austere and precise admissions criteria that ensure only Christian students from Christian families are enrolled to attend classes taught by Christian teachers. The question I have for K. C. is very simple: *When and how did the covenantal Christian school ever provide you with opportunities to interact with the world?* Steve came to the covenantal Christian school "to find God" and became a student chaplain in the covenantal Christian school. While that is a great honor and affirmation of the Christian nurture in his life, it still locates Steve's ministry inside "the huddle."

Corien celebrated the effectiveness of the covenantal Christian school because her son was equipped "to analyze and evaluate the world around him." I agree that the covenantal Christian schools may be positioned to provide instruction that produces this quality—but Deuteronomy chapter 6 is quite specific that the parents are responsible for the discipleship of their children. The institutions that have been established by God to disciple children are the family and the church—not the school. While Mark rightly describes this process as one that partners with parents, I suspect that there are far more parents who surrender this role to the covenantal school than who actively participate in the discipleship process.

In many cases, families in a covenantal Christian school live in an environment that bears little resemblance to Jesus' model of discipleship. The "careful exposure" that Mark describes is unidimensional as it only deals with the educational process. Jesus' discipleship process unfolded in real-time. In Matthew 15:21, for example, Jesus took His disciples to the Gentile region of Tyre and Sidon—a pagan region where observant Jewish folk did not typically go—as part of their training as His followers. The covenantal Christian school so closely monitors a Christian student's environment that, when they encounter the foreign culture of secular society, they tend to respond with right answers stated in judgmental ways. An overload of the "right" information does not ensure a transformation of heart.

Furthermore, it has become increasingly clear that Christian schooling does not necessarily do a better job when it comes to academics. In a recent study of fourth- to eighth-grade students, children from conservative Christian schools fared *the same* as public school students in most areas and performed *below* public school students in mathematics, when compared with similar students.[1]

As parents looking to educate our children, we must employ the most effective means to give our children the opportunity to achieve. Each child is uniquely designed and created by God. I have two daughters who have completely opposite personalities. Both have unique needs and talents. As they have grown, their needs have changed. As parents, we must understand the diversity of God's creation and recognize that, for many Christians, public schooling remains their best option.

Response by G. Tyler Fisher
Perspective of Open-Admission Christian Schooling

The best way to describe my reaction to the bulk of this essay is agreement. It is difficult to find places where it should be critiqued. Given that fact, I suppose that I should offer some explanation. Christian schooling operates on a continuum. I stand stridently against rigid, cloistered closed-admissions Christian schools that function as if they have no responsibilities for their communities and to the world. Students that come from these schools—schools often motivated by a desire to avoid worldliness—are ill-prepared to live a life of transformative faith in fellowship with other believers. They lack intellectual curiosity,

---

1. http://nces.ed.gov/nationsreportcard/pubs/studies/2006461.asp#section2

and they have been catechized in ways that will be obsolete two seconds after graduation.

Thankfully, Mark Eckel's chapter rightly opposes this sort of education. Bravo! The author also has his students reading good and bad philosophers. Plus, he quotes Wendell Berry. What more could I ask? He criticizes open-admissions schools because there is a danger of those schools trying to please everyone. This I willingly admit, but I note that my approach is a very guarded open-admission approach. So, I am in agreement with almost everything in this chapter. We have almost identical goals at my school concerning what we want to accomplish with our students.

I do, however, still detect a couple of pertinent differences between the Christian schooling for everyone approach and the Christian schools for Christian families approach. While I mention them here, I want to recognize at the outset that these objections do not describe all covenantal Christian schools.

The greatest contention is where the Christian responsibility ends. Many covenantal schools unwittingly fall into a trap—a ghetto—where we can live peaceably and contentedly among our own kind while the cares and concerns of the community are left for others. I am not content with such an attitude because I do not believe that Christ is content with such an attitude. I will not cede one inch anywhere to secular learning. And, while I will guard the environment and admissions of my school judiciously, I long for the day when all children in our country receive a Christian education and when the philosophy that now drives public education is recognized as bankrupt.

I believe that our responsibilities as believers do not come to an end until all the poor are cared for, until every person has heard the gospel, and until all have access to schools that teach a coherent worldview. Even in this last longing I am particularly concerned with the poor who cannot now afford such a coherent education. The Nicene Creed says that Jesus Christ "for us men, and for our salvation, came down from heaven." He did not leave us to our own devices; He came to us and for us. Christ has won the battle over death and hell. His victory resounds from an empty tomb. While we must be wise as serpents and harmless as doves, our approach ever since Pentecost is to be on the offensive, not the defensive. We need fear no darkness. And, until we live in this victory and take the cares of our culture and the needs of the neediest upon ourselves, we will never have the impact on the culture that we desire.

Covenantal schools restrict enrollment to believing families. My question is, Should they? Is it biblically necessary to do so? While I applaud their diligence, I do not believe that church membership or a profession of faith is a necessary bar on the door of the school. The school is not a church with holy ordinances to be safeguarded. Though Christian schools must be diligent to guard their admissions choices and their environment, they may have a greater cultural impact if they judiciously open the doors a little wider.

Response by Michael S. Wilder
Perspective of Homeschooling

Christian parents face a fork in the road when making educational decisions. They are confronted with two signs. One directs them toward public education based on unbiblical perspectives. The other sign points toward a Christ-centered education. As I read through Mark Eckel's chapter, it is clear that we agree philosophically about educating children in a setting where Christian truth is foundational and integral to the process. Mark clearly advocates Christian schooling in a Christian context for Christian families.

Mark differentiates covenantal Christian schooling from open-admission Christian schooling by emphasizing the importance of the Christian school and Christian parents partnering together. He suggests that the intent of this partnering is to develop the next generation of believers, to train children in a biblical worldview, and to provide a biblical framework that builds God-centered purpose into every part of life. I wholeheartedly agree.

He also sees that a child's education is preparation for life. He suggests that covenantal Christian schooling is the best way to prepare believers for cultural engagement and cultural transformation. Mark views Christian teachers as the school's "living curriculum," and I resonate with this descriptor. It is a perfect way to emphasize the necessity of a student being exposed to a teacher who models godly thinking, emotions, and behaviors.

Lest anyone think I agree with everything that Mark has stated, let me clarify where I believe he is guilty of overstatement in his argument. According to Mark Eckel, covenantal Christian schooling offers children an educational experience that is focused far more precisely on what matters than any other educational option; covenantal schooling offers meaning, permanence, and a precious heritage.

When Mark speaks of "meaning," he raises the issues of *time, place,* and *people.* Let's look at these. First, the issue of *time.* Eckel acknowledges the vast amount of time that a child spends in school in the course of the academic year—approximately seven hours per day, 180 days per year. This is an incredible amount of time—much of which is wasted in the daily schedules of many schools, while the typical homeschooler completes her work in about three hours in the elementary grades and five hours or so in the middle and high school years. Mark does remind the reader that the amount of time spent in the educational enterprise does not necessarily guarantee effectiveness, and he rightly recognizes the importance of where and with whom the time is spent. And yet, when it comes to the issue of *place,* I contend that there is still no place like home to invest this time in the best possible way to train your child in a holistic manner seeking intellectual, emotional, physical, and spiritual transformation.

As for the issue of *people,* I strongly suggest that the parent remains the optimal educational choice. Parents know what motivates their children, what interests them, and what environment leads to the most effective learning experience. When Mark references his response to some friends—"Most homeschooling parents do not have your educational backgrounds or your support network"—he makes the mistake of implying that parents may not be qualified to teach their children. The fact is that more than three-fourths of homeschooling parents have attended college or vocational training while 44.4 percent have earned baccalaureate or graduate degrees. When you consider this statistic alongside the ready availability of computer technology and homeschooling cooperatives, Mark's argument begins to melt away. And for those who believe state certification for homeschooling parents is a must, the data demonstrate that children perform at about the same academic level, regardless of whether or not the teacher has been certified as a teacher. Simply put, Mark overstates his position when he raises the issue of time, place, and people. I would suggest that homeschooling conducted by godly parents would not only demonstrate the same positive Christian characteristics as a covenantal school, but that it would also model what happens when everyone is not on their best behavior—how a Christian lives life in a potentially "messy" environment.

Mark discusses the passing on of a precious heritage from one generation to another. When it comes to godly heritage, the family is the place where, according to Scripture, the passing on of a precious heritage occurs most readily. When applied to the heritage of ideas that he discusses, I am supportive of those great ideas being preserved and taught in the educational context and particularly from a Christian perspective. Yet, it is overreaching to suggest that the best place for that to happen is in a covenantal school. In our home and in many others, the curriculum focuses heavily on literature and on history of ideas.

Nevertheless, I end by affirming Mark's clarity and vision concerning what makes a covenantal school a viable option for Christian parents. If all covenantal schools in America followed the principles he has outlined, God's people would be equipped to stand stronger for truth.

Counter-Response by Mark Eckel
Perspective of Covenantal Christian Schooling

"Ghettos" or "huddles" are metaphors used by my colleagues to communicate their concerns about covenantal Christian schooling. They are right on one point: There *is* a separation between the covenantal Christian school and the culture within which it operates. Beliefs and teachers must be distinctively Christian. Put another way, it is vital for the players in my "huddle" to be on my team.

"Ghettos" can be neighborhoods where everyone sticks together. But to dispel the negative stereotype, let me say that covenantal Christian schools are not necessarily closed to the culture or to concern for people in their community. The Christian schools with which I have had the honor to serve have carried out service ministries in local and international contexts. Doug Howard at Lenawee Christian School in Adrian, Michigan, for instance, has established a service club ministry called "Project Build." This ministry is now heading a new outreach that has a worldwide impact. And I maintain that critical, Christian engagement of the culture is woven within the apologetic framework of covenantal Christian schools as they demonstrate deliberate concern for demolishing "strongholds" and other arguments, especially when the philosophies of the world are empty and deceptive (2 Cor 10:4–5; Col 2:8).

Covenantal Christian schools are ignorant neither of cultural needs nor how to meet them. Rather than focusing on external fixes such as "stop smoking" or "say 'no' to drugs," covenantal schools train students that ideas have consequences. The internal orientation and character development of a Christian student is foremost in a covenantal school: thoughts, attitudes, and actions must correspond to what is good (Titus 3:1,8,14). Students who are doctrinally prepared to engage the culture in winsome ways will demonstrate through words and deeds the distinctiveness of the Christian viewpoint (Col 4:5–6; 1 Thess 4:11–12; Titus 2:1–10).

It is this very mind-set that also sets covenantal Christian schools apart from homeschooling. No amount of parental credentialing or earned degrees, whether Christian or pagan, necessarily qualifies one for instructional success. All of us, Christian parents included, bring with us our own insular assumptions about life—and mere use of outside technologies is not sufficient to broaden students' perspectives. And that is why no better place exists to train the next generation of Christian children than with Christian teachers covenanting together for the sake of their students.

While each writer strongly contends for their point of view in this book, make no mistake about what unifies our commitment. We believe that Jesus' message of life is the only change agent that will right all wrongs in our world. Together we stand, committed to the gospel that must be proclaimed to every creature with Christ supreme in all things, while teaching everyone in the wisdom to which we have committed our lives (Col 1:13–14,18,23,28–29).

CHAPTER 7

There's Still No Place like Home
WHY HOMESCHOOLING WORKS

By Michael S. Wilder

Every enduring movie includes at least a few well-known and oft-repeated lines. This holds true for several movies released in 1939. That year's list of movies included *Mr. Smith Goes to Washington, Of Mice and Men, Gone with the Wind,* and of course *The Wizard of Oz.* Although *The Wizard of Oz* lost to *Gone with the Wind* that year at the Academy Awards, the Technicolor scenes will forever be imprinted in the minds of many generations of children.

I am not the best at quoting movie lines from memory, yet even I remember Dorothy's first and last lines in the Land of Oz: "Toto, I've a feeling we're not in Kansas anymore," she said upon her arrival in Oz. Then, as she clicked her ruby red slippers, she repeated, "There's no place like home. There's no place like home."

In Oz, Dorothy found herself in an unfamiliar land where everything seemed so different, so out of place, so confusing. She desperately desired someplace where the foundations of her life were a little surer. And so, she whispered, "There's no place like home."

That is still true, you know.

In a culture where so much is so out of place and where educational values seem in constant flux, there really is no place like home to train your child—and this includes not only your child's education in Scripture but also your child's schooling for life.

Perhaps you are reading this book because you are concerned about your children's schooling. That concern has driven you to pursue the best possible educational option for your family. As a Christian, you want to provide the educational opportunity that meets your child's needs in the best possible way while producing godly character and a distinctly Christian worldview.

As you consider the educational options for your family, I encourage you to reflect on the following questions: "Who is responsible for my child's education?" "What is the goal of education?" and, "How should my Christian beliefs influence my educational decisions?"

As you consider these questions, allow me to take a moment to tell you about my family's journey to homeschooling. I choose the word "journey" intentionally because it was indeed a journey. When our children were younger, we placed them in preschool at a church where I served as one of the pastors. Ginger and I made this choice because it exposed our children to a formal learning environment and because it was free. A couple years later, we relocated and enrolled our oldest daughter Daly in the local public school; our younger daughters Ashton and McKenzie soon followed.

For three years, my wife and I involved ourselves in parent-teacher organizations and in the children's classrooms. We volunteered and worked to build relationships with the faculty and administration. The principal and many teachers were Christians. With the exception of one teacher who seemed obsessed with cognitive development at the expense of all other dimensions of life, we were satisfied with this experience.

While dealing with some dissatisfaction over that particular teacher, I was reading a book entitled *Philosophy and Education* by George Knight. Part of what I read caused me to reconsider my willingness to place our children in public schools. There are two pages early in Knight's book that provoked this reconsideration.

In one section, Knight discusses the role of the school as a partner in the educational process. I remember writing in the margin of that page, "Can a secular school be an appropriate partner?" Several pages later, he asked why Christians are willing to spend millions of dollars each year on private systems of education when public school systems are freely available. Here is how he answered that question:

> It is because of their metaphysical beliefs regarding the nature of ultimate reality, the existence of God, the role of God in human affairs, and the nature and role of human beings as God's children. Men and women, at their deepest level, are motivated by metaphysical beliefs. They are willing to live and die for these convictions, and they desire to create educational environments in which these most basic beliefs will be taught to their children.[1]

Knight is accurate in stating that we are deeply motivated by metaphysical beliefs—that is to say, by our convictions about what is ultimately real. His words prompted my wife and me to rethink our core beliefs and to commit ourselves to Christian education for our children.

The journey toward homeschooling continued when we moved to Louisville, Kentucky. A commitment to Christian education meant that we had three options: A Christian academy, homeschooling, or some hybrid of the two. I had attended public school, and I strongly opposed homeschooling. My wife had attended public and Christian schools through eighth grade before being homeschooled in high school, so she was open to the possibility of home education.

In the end, we placed our children in a local Christian academy. By year's end, we were disenchanted. One teacher did not seem to be concerned with developing children as whole people—as people who are growing spiritually, socially, emotionally, and cognitively. Clear disparity existed between the school's

1. G. Knight, *Philosophy and Education* (Berrien Springs, Mich.: Andrews University Press, 1998), 17.

theoretical biblical worldview and actual classroom practices. Coordination of faith with learning was inadequate. We also began to see the degree to which our children could potentially benefit from one-on-one instruction.

These issues converged that spring, and we committed to homeschooling our children for the following school year. As I write these words, the third year of homeschooling in the Wilder household has just begun. We did not begin with an ideological commitment to Christian education, and we certainly did not begin with a passion for homeschooling. It came as the result of a journey, and it provides a unique perspective on the process.

Interestingly, I find that our family's pathway is similar to many other homeschooling families. Their commitment to homeschooling emerged slowly as they wrestled with the best options for educating their children. My present prediction is that, in the near future, the number of families opting for homeschooling will multiply. This prediction carries no prophetic authority, yet I believe it to be firmly founded in well-documented trends. To comprehend the context of contemporary education, let us look at a few of those trends.

Trends in Homeschooling

In 1999 and 2003, the National Center for Educational Statistics (NCES) collected data to be used to estimate the number of homeschool students in the United States. The data from the 1999 survey suggested that at that time there were approximately 850,000 children in the United States who were schooled partly or exclusively at home. This number represented 1.7 percent of the school-aged population at that time.

By 2003, the number of homeschoolers had increased to 1,096,000 students out of a total student population of 50 million—2.2 percent of the school-aged population. Of these homeschooled students, 82 percent were schooled only at home. Twelve and one-half percent were enrolled in school outside the home less than nine hours a week, and a little more than 5.5 percent were enrolled in a school outside the home between nine and twenty-five hours each week.[2] Brian Ray, president of the National Home Education Research Institute, estimated in 2009 that between 2 million and 2.5 million children had been home educated during the 2007-2008 academic year. He also said the method was growing quickly in popularity among minorities, with about 15 percent of homeschool families being non-Anglo.[3] Even though this is still a small percentage compared to the total population, it is large enough to indicate that home education is becoming much more accepted among American families.

Why Do Parents Choose Home Education?

Why are growing numbers of parents making the choice to educate at home? Researchers have typically split the homeschool population into two groups: *ideologues* and *pedagogues*. Some parents value certain beliefs or virtues, and they do not see these beliefs or virtues being adequately or correctly communicated in traditional school settings. These parents are referred to as *ideologues*.

Other parents view the teaching methods used in traditional schools as inadequate. These parents are *pedagogues*. Pedagogically-motivated parents remove their children from traditional school because of the school's perceived methodological incompetence, not because of any supposed heretical content in the school's curriculum.[4]

While somewhat helpful, I believe that this twofold description is far from satisfactory. As I examine the data, I find *four* motivating factors for homeschooling. Furthermore, I suggest that most parents have one primary motive for homeschooling that is accompanied by several secondary motives. The four motivating factors that seem to form the foundations for the choice to educate at home are (1) *environment*, (2) *ideology*, (3) *pedagogy*, and (4) *lifestyle*.

In 2003, NCES researchers asked homeschooling parents whether particular reasons for selecting home education applied

2. National Center for Educational Statistics, *Homeschooling in the United States: 2003:* http://nces.ed.gov.

3. E. Roach, "Homeschooling numbers climb 36% since 2003" (January 12, 2009): http://www.bpnews.org.

4. J. Van Galen, "Ideology, Curriculum, Pedagogy in Home Education," *Education and Urban Society* 21 (1988): 52–68.

to them. Parents then identified which of these particular reasons were most important. Here are the results of this research:[5]

Reasons for Choosing Homeschooling	Applicable	Most Important
Concern about environment of other schools	85.4%	31.2%
Desire to provide religious or moral instruction	72.3%	29.8%
Dissatisfaction with academic instruction at other schools	68.2%	16.5%
Other reasons (child's choice, flexibility, control over curriculum)	20.1%	8.8%
Child has other special needs	28.9%	7.2%
Child has a physical or mental health problem	15.9%	6.5%

Environmentally Motivated Home Education. According to this report, parents were most concerned about their children's environment—that is, conditions and influences in the schools that could affect their children negatively. These environmental factors include protecting children from bullying, violence, drugs, and gangs. Other concerns, including antisocial influences and sexual discrimination, could also be included.[6]

There is good reason to be concerned about environmental factors, especially in public schools. According to a joint study from the Department of Education and the Department of Justice, victimization rates of students between twelve and eighteen years of age declined in public schools between 1992 and 2005. While that is good news, it is not much comfort in light of the other statistics in the study. During the 2005–06 academic year, around 1.5 million students were victimized in some way while at school. These acts of violence inside our nation's public schools

5. National Center for Educational Statistics, *Homeschooling in the United States: 2003:* http://nces.ed.gov.

6. K. Nemar, *Understanding Education,* June 2002. Occasional paper number 48 (National Center for the Study of Privatization and Education, Teachers College, Columbia University).

included 868,100 thefts and 628,200 violent crimes. The violent crimes ranged from simple assault to rape and even murder.[7]

Preliminary data show that among youth ages 5–18, there were 17 school-associated violent deaths from July 1, 2005, through June 30, 2006 (14 homicides and 3 suicides). . . . During the 2005–06 school year, 86 percent of public schools reported that at least one violent crime, theft, or other crime occurred at their school. In 2005, 8 percent of students in grades 9–12 reported being threatened or injured with a weapon in the previous 12 months, and 25 percent reported that drugs were made available to them on school property. In the same year, 28 percent of students ages 12–18 reported having been bullied at school during the previous 6 months.[8]

Think about these numbers for a moment. One out of every twelve students will be threatened or injured with a weapon while in attendance at a public school. One out of every four children will be offered drugs or bullied on school grounds. These types of statistics ought to cause any parent to consider carefully whether they should be willing to place their offspring in this type of schooling environment.

Ideologically Motivated Home Education. The 2003 NCES report also suggested that nearly three-fourths of the time parents were concerned about their children's religious or moral training. These parents fit into the category of *ideologues.* Studies suggest that many ideological homeschoolers are Christians.[9] Yet Christians are far from the only ideologues. Out of curiosity, I did Internet searches on Jewish homeschooling, Islamic homeschooling, Buddhist homeschooling, and even pagan and atheist homeschooling. Without exception, each of these searches resulted in page after page of links.

---

7. National Center for Educational Statistics, *Indicators of School Crime and Safety: 2007:* http://nces.ed.gov.

8. Ibid.

9. B. Ray, *Strengths of Their Own* (Salem, Ore.: NHERI, 1997); Van Galen, "Ideology, Curriculum, Pedagogy in Home Education," 52–68.

Pedagogically Motivated Home Education. Increasing numbers of parents are dissatisfied with academic instruction in traditional schools. The reasons reported for their dissatisfaction range from overall low-quality instruction to specific methods of teaching employed by teachers, inadequate support for children with special needs, or inadequate personal attention given to the student.

Lifestyle-Motivated Home Education. The final motivation that moves many parents to educate at home is *lifestyle.* Lifestyle factors include issues related to family structure, schedule, or life-situations. Perhaps one parent travels extensively for his or her job and takes the family. Maybe the child excels in a particular sport and homeschooling permits a more flexible schedule for training. It may be that parents want to place their children in a private school, but they are financially unable. Regardless of the initial motives for home education, parents often continue homeschooling for reasons other than their original motive.[10]

Characteristics of Homeschooling Families

What sorts of people choose to homeschool? Most often, homeschool families in the United States are two-parent households (80.8%) with a larger number of children than average (three or more children, 62%). More than three-fourths of homeschooling parents have attended college or vocational training, with 44.4% having earned a baccalaureate or graduate degree. Most homeschoolers are Christian, though the proportion of families from other religious backgrounds is steadily increasing.[11] A higher percentage of the homeschooling population lives in the South (40.6%) than in the West (22.3%), Midwest (21.8%), or Northeast (15.3%).[12]

At this point, some of you may find yourselves saying, "We don't fit the typical profile for a homeschooling family. Perhaps

---

10. J. Knowles, "The Context of Home Schooling in the United States," *Education and Urban Society* 21 (1988): 5–15.

11. B. Ray, "Home-schoolers on to College," *The Journal of College Admission* (Fall 2004): 5–11.

12. National Center for Educational Statistics, *Homeschooling in the United States: 2003:* http://nces.ed.gov.

we shouldn't even consider it." I admit that it is probably easier for two-parent families with one parent in the labor force to homeschool. Still, even if your situation does not afford this opportunity, I encourage you not to reject homeschooling automatically. There are families of all descriptions who are making it work.

I am thinking of a single mom named Kathy. Her two sons attended public school during most of their elementary years while Kathy worked as a financial analyst. Her frustration with her sons' lack of academic progress and with what she perceived as poor pedagogy led her to seek other options. As she plotted a new course for her children's education, she became very entrepreneurial. Kathy began a home-based business to produce written family histories. This new business now allows Kathy to preserve her mornings for homeschooling. When business slows down, she supplements her income by providing typing services for law firms and even by playing the piano at a local funeral home. Her sons have flourished in this new learning environment, and Kathy is convinced that she made the right decision.[13] Home education works well for two-parent, one-income families, but it can also work for children from a broad range of other backgrounds.

Homeschooling from Cradle to College

In the last few months, several friends have been blessed with the births of new babies. Those early days of life can prompt deep reflection on the parts of dads and moms. As they consider the incredible responsibility God has given them, some even initiate conversations about how to educate their children.

Because our friends know that we homeschool, they sometimes ask us about this. It is a delight for us to answer these questions, because it reminds us why we are on this journey with our children. Such conversations remind us that, despite the difficult days, there are many more good weeks than bad as we seek to train our children for God's glory.

---

13. http://www.homeschooloasis.com/art_single_mom_hs.htm

So why have we chosen to homeschool? Before I answer that question, I want to look first at a wider question of who is really responsible for your child's education. From a broad historical perspective, the answer seems mixed. Some societies have expected families to take direct responsibility for their children's education. Others have seen education as the responsibility of the local community or of some larger social entity. Viewed from a relatively recent American perspective, the answer seems less mixed: In the United States, the state has assumed the primary responsibility for schooling children.

And how did this responsibility shift to the state?

In 1852, the state of Massachusetts established the first compulsory education attendance law in the United States. This statute required children to attend "common school" at least twelve weeks each year. A few other states soon implemented similar laws, but they did not stringently enforce their statutes. By 1918, however, all forty-eight states had established compulsory attendance statutes, and many states were enforcing these laws. Between the Great Depression and the Baby Boom, enforcement intensified until, not long after the midpoint of the twentieth century, a state-sponsored education was assumed not only for elementary children but also for adolescents.

Some have argued that industrialization and immigration necessitated compulsory education laws. According to these individuals, a public school system was necessary to mold diverse cultures and social strata into a democratic society with a common set of values. Whether or not the public school system was necessary, it certainly transformed the American educational landscape. Today, the vast majority of American children—approximately 50 million students total—attend public schools in the United States.[14] This radical shift has moved education from a familial responsibility to a state responsibility. At the dawning of the twenty-first century, five generations of Americans have now been educated predominantly in state-sponsored schools. As a result, many parents assume that education is the government's responsibility.

---

14. http://nces.ed.gov/programs/coe/2008/section1/table.asp?tableID=858

Educational Responsibility in Biblical Perspective

What does Scripture have to say about such assumptions? The answer seems quite evident as I read the words of Moses spoken to the nation of Israel:

> Listen, Israel: The LORD our God, the LORD is One. Love the LORD your God with all your heart, with all your soul, and with all your strength. These words that I am giving you today are to be in your heart. Repeat them to your children. Talk about them when you sit in your house and when you walk along the road, when you lie down and when you get up. Bind them as a sign on your hand and let them be a symbol on your forehead. Write them on the doorposts of your house and on your gates. (Deut 6:4–9)

Moses clearly informed Israelite parents that they were personally responsible to disciple and teach their children. Moses included a methodological directive, stating that this process of discipling and teaching must be integrated throughout the activities of daily life. He even told parents to prepare themselves to answer their children's day-to-day questions in God-centered ways. Asaph the psalmist made much the same point:

> My people, hear my instruction; listen to what I say. I will declare wise sayings; I will speak mysteries from the past—things we have heard and known and that our fathers have passed down to us. We must not hide them from their children, but must tell a future generation the praises of the LORD, His might, and the wonderful works He has performed. He established a testimony in Jacob and set up a law in Israel, which He commanded our fathers to teach to their children so that a future generation—children yet to be born—might know. They were to rise and tell their children so that they might put their confidence in God and not forget God's works, but keep His commands. Then they would not be like their fathers, a stubborn and rebellious generation, a generation whose heart was not loyal and whose spirit was not faithful to God. (Ps 78:1–8)

The New Testament expresses similar expectations. The apostle Paul told fathers in the church at Ephesus, "don't stir up anger in your children, but bring them up in the training and instruction of the Lord" (Eph 6:4).

Discipleship, Learning, Education, and Schooling in Theological Perspective

Some read the verses I cited above, along with other texts such as Proverbs 3:1; 22:6; and 2 Timothy 1:5; 3:15, and agree that parents are primarily responsible for discipling their children. Yet these same persons will argue that parents do not bear primary responsibility for the formal education of their children. I am puzzled by such thinking. Discipleship is a process of development wherein Christians are transformed and become more committed followers of Jesus. The results of discipleship include transformation of knowledge, behaviors, and attitudes so that the child reflects the character and identity of Jesus.

If discipleship includes not only spiritual transformation but also transformation in the way children think, it seems absurd for parents to see themselves as responsible for their children's "spiritual development" while relinquishing to others responsibilities for the development of children's minds. Spiritual development is inseparable from cognitive and affective growth.

That is why I view *education* as a subset of *learning* and *learning* as a subset of *discipleship*. Discipleship is the larger category of which learning is one part, and education represents a specific form of learning. Learning is a process of gaining knowledge that leads to changes in thinking, feeling, or doing. Learning "is not limited to an institutional context. . . . Learning is a lifelong process that may occur at any time and any place."[15] Education is distinguishable as a subset of learning because education functions with some specific goal. It is *directed learning.*[16] Discipleship is a broader category than learning because discipleship includes not only directed learning but also learning through the

---

15. Knight, *Philosophy and Education,* 10.
16. Ibid.

experiences of daily life. Discipleship is a whole-life event that cannot be confined to certain days or times.

At this point, you may be asking where schooling fits. I suggest that schooling is *formal, directed learning with specific educational goals*. Schooling is a form of education, education is a directed form of learning, and learning is a form of discipleship. Schooling transmits specific knowledge that students will need to become functional adults. Viewed from a Christian perspective, schooling should include not only information about the world but also knowledge of the Creator and patterns of thinking that fit all knowledge into a biblical worldview.

Now if schooling is part of education, if education is part of learning, and if learning is part of discipleship for life, then going to school must be viewed as part of a larger discipleship process. For good or for bad, your children are being discipled through their schooling. If you send your child to public school, he is most likely being discipled in a vague secularism that, by educating without any reference to God, implies that it is possible to grow into a whole and healthy adult without God.

In too many cases, Christian parents in the United States have turned over the responsibility for their children's teaching and discipleship to professionals. The church is expected to deal with children's spiritual and social needs, and the school is expected to build the child's mind. In this way, parents fail to obey the biblical mandate that calls us to train our sons and daughters. This failure is not typically rooted in rebellion but in misunderstanding. This misunderstanding has grown out of the separation of schooling from discipleship—a separation that has allowed Christians to turn over the curricular content of their child's education to a system that rejects a Christian worldview. That is why some prominent Christian leaders have called for an "exit strategy" from public schools.[17]

Facing the Fork

When talking to parents who are wrestling with educational decisions, here is the point where I say, "And this brings us to the

---

17. R. A. Mohler, *Culture Shift* (Colorado Springs, Colo.: Multnomah, 2008), 65–72.

fork in the road." Two signs stand in front of us. One directs us toward education that is based on an unbiblical perspective, and the other sign points students toward a Christ-centered education that places every part of life within a biblical worldview.

Both roads may lead to graduates who are "successful," according to the world's standards of success. But if learning and education are viewed within the larger context of discipleship, is worldly success really the purpose of education? Not if education and schooling are seen as elements within a framework of Christian discipleship! Both roads can produce citizens who will contribute to earthly communities, but is that the ultimate goal of schooling? Not if schooling is part of discipleship. Both roads may yield "functional adults"—but I desire so much more for my children than societal functionality.

To develop a robust Christian worldview, it is not enough for a child to learn the Christian Scriptures. Children must be trained to examine science, math, and humanities within a biblical framework. And this training cannot be confined to a few minutes each morning or evening that you as a parent add to the secular education your children may receive throughout the day.

That is why I must take the road that trains children in a biblical worldview throughout every part of their educational experience. If you as a parent take this pathway with me, you are quickly faced with an additional fork in the road. This decision has to do with *where* your children will be trained in this biblical worldview. Will it be the Christian academy or the Christian homeschool?

I readily admit that some Christian academies do excel at developing a biblical worldview in children. Yet others fail miserably because their teachers have little or no biblical training and have no methodological training for coordinating faith with learning.

Does that then mean the only viable option is Christian homeschooling? I do not think so; as I said earlier, there are some Christian academies that do well. Still, even in those situations, I must challenge Christian parents with this thought: During the school year, your children will spend at least *30 percent* of their waking hours in some educational context. If you are ultimately responsible for discipling them, why would you *not* desire to spend those hours with your child? Those who teach my children have the greatest impact how my children's worldview is shaped. If I am responsible before God for the discipleship of my children, I want my wife and myself to be the primary influencers in my children's lives.

How Homeschooling Works

After my wife and I talk with others about the *why* of Christian education and homeschooling, there is usually a follow-up conversation. At this point, people begin to ask questions that begin with *how* instead of *why:* How do I plan the best approach? How do I select curriculum? How do I navigate legal issues? How do I negotiate college admissions?

Being Honest about Your Motives

I suggest that your first step toward answering the *how* questions should be to examine your motives. Be honest. Is your primary reason for home education *environmental, ideological, pedagogical,* or *lifestyle related?* After you have answered this question, recognize this simple fact: Any of these motives, taken to the extreme, can produce negative results. For example, if your primary motive is to protect your child from a negative environment, you could run the risk of isolating your child so completely that she does not learn to respond constructively to her culture. If your motive has to do with ideology, you might find yourself structuring the curriculum so that the child only hears ideas from Christian sources. Though the desire to shield children from anti-Christian ideas is understandable, the development of a biblical worldview requires that the child also learn to comprehend and to critique alternative perspectives. As children increase in maturity, their exposure to unbiblical ideas should increase proportionately and purposefully.

Suppose that your prime motive is because of poor pedagogy in traditional schools: For the sake of your child's future learning

Approaches and Curriculum in Homeschooling

- **Traditional approach.** Those using the traditional approach will typically follow a specified scope and sequence of material from a specific publisher. Boxed curriculum that includes textbooks, study schedules, and workbooks might need to be purchased.
- **Classical approach.** This approach is rooted in the liberal arts and dates back to the Middle Ages. The classical approach is structured around trivium (grammar, logic, rhetoric), quadrivium (arithmetic, geometry, music, and astronomy), and the advanced study of philosophy and theology. The classical approach in homeschooling would begin with the trivium, which would include a preparatory stage where the child would learn basic reading, writing, and arithmetic. This would lead to the grammar stage, which emphasizes the use of language to express thought. This, in turn, would be followed by the logic stage, which focuses on developing the student's ability to think and reason well. The final stage of the trivium would be reached during high school years as the student develops the skill of rhetoric—the use of language to persuade and to instruct.
- **Technological approach.** The last decade has seen great advances in video-based and Internet-based learning. Parents can now access virtual tutors, virtual schools, and highly developed online curriculum. The three most obvious advantages to this approach include learner access to experts in a given field of study, preparation of the learner for future collegiate online studies, and the development of learner independence.
- **Unit studies approach.** This approach involves taking a theme or topic in which a child has great interest and exploring it over an extended period of time. This approach intentionally integrates the various subject areas like history, language, arts, science, math, reading, and spelling as the topic is examined. The advantage to this approach is its recognition that learning is typically heightened when the subject matter intersects with the learner's interest.
- **Charlotte Mason approach.** Adherents to this approach believe the children learn best through active participation and should be given the opportunity to play, create, and be involved in real-life circumstances. Students learn subjects such as geography, history,

and literature from "living books" (books that make subject matter come to life) and experience engaging field trips like visits to museums and regular nature walks. Learning evaluation is based on the student's ability to discuss and narrate the subject matter, rather than through testing.

- **Unschooling approach.** This approach assumes that children are naturally curious and desirous of learning. This assumption translates into child initiated learning—the child determines what they are interested in studying and are encouraged to discover truths for themselves. Unschoolers do not have a regimented curriculum or schedule and primarily learn through life experience.

Some parents also combine one or more of these approaches. Rather than purchasing boxed curriculum, they are more likely to select individual pieces that reflect the needs and interests of their children in areas such as math, reading, and language arts, while perhaps taking an unschooling approach for other subject areas.

in college, be certain that he gains the capacity to learn through methods other than your particular approach. If your motive is lifestyle related, and especially if your homeschooling is less structured, do not forget to train your child to function well in both less-structured *and* more-structured environments.

Setting Up the Right Structure

How you structure your homeschool depends on your chosen curriculum and approach. If your family needs more structure, you might set up rigid time schedules, a miniature classroom, and even specified dates for testing. You might be best served by selecting traditional, classical, or technological curriculum for your children (see the sidebar for more information about each of these educational options).

If on the other hand your family opts for more flexibility, you may be more comfortable with the Charlotte Mason approach, or a unit studies emphasis. These approaches allow your child to adjust and to develop curriculum that responds to her needs and interests.

Another question you will face as you structure your children's homeschooling experience is who will be responsible for daily teaching. Usually, one parent will embrace primary responsibility for teaching. In many homes, however, this task will be shared between the parents based on their particular areas of expertise. In some cases, the parent who serves as a primary teacher may have one day off each week. If that is the case, the secondary teacher might teach on that day, providing the other parent with a day of rest and preparation. Other homeschooling families join cooperative educational programs designed specifically to strengthen home education. Typically "homeschool cooperatives" meet a day or two each week. Parents choose courses to fit their children's interests and needs. Sometimes, the cooperatives hire special instructors; in other cases, parents with expertise in particular areas serve as volunteer teachers.

Navigating Legal Issues

From a legal perspective, the good news is that all fifty of the United States deem homeschooling to be legal. Each state does have different regulations, though. Perhaps the best way to understand these regulations is to look at four categories:[18]

- *States requiring no notice.* Parents are not required to initiate any contact with educational authorities, but they may be required to keep attendance records.
- *States with low regulation.* Here the state requires that parents notify the state or the local school district.
- *States with moderate regulation.* This is where the state requires parents to send notifications, test scores, and/or professional evaluations of student progress to the state or local school district.
- *States with high regulation.* Some states require parents to send notification, achievement test scores, and/or professional evaluations of student progress, plus there may be other requirements. For example, individuals from the state or the school district might ask to approve the

---

18. http://www.hslda.org/laws/default.asp

curriculum, to determine whether the parent is qualified to teach, or to make home visits.

Even if the state does not require records, it is wise to maintain documentation of each child's learning. To assist you in navigating the legal issues, it is important to be aware of organizations such as the Home School Legal Defense Association (HSLDA) and other groups that can provide legal information and representation for homeschoolers.

Negotiating College Admission

Increasing numbers of colleges recognize that more and more homeschoolers are applying to their institutions. Many colleges and universities have crafted policies specifically for the admission of homeschooled students. Some colleges are even actively recruiting these students because of their academic excellence— and they should! After all, homeschooled students typically score between fifteen and thirty percentile points higher than average public school students on standardized tests.[19]

Raising Objections

By now, I hope you recognize homeschooling as a viable option for your family. I must admit, though, that I would be disappointed if you were not also raising some questions, and perhaps even some objections. I have raised a few objections myself over the years—remember, at one time, I was utterly opposed to homeschooling our daughters! So what are the objections to home education? As I read and interact with parents and educators, I consistently hear three significant objections to homeschooling: (1) Parents are not qualified teachers, (2) the children experience inadequate socialization, and (3) there is a lack of fervor for reaching the world with the gospel. Let us look carefully at each potential point of difficulty.

---

19. Ray, "Homeschoolers on to College," 5–11.

Are Parents Qualified Teachers?

Can a parent really be a qualified teacher? I resonate strongly with a concern for qualified teaching. Much of my time is spent in a seminary, educating current and future church leaders. Part of my job is to make certain that students become qualified teachers in schools and congregations. Still, I am convinced that the average parent is qualified to teach his or her children.

The reason for this is that parents often understand the nature and needs of their children better than a schoolteacher. A teacher may meet a child on the first day of the school year and spend only nine months with him or her. Furthermore, parents are in a better position to know what intrinsically motivates and interests their children. This knowledge equips parents to select teaching methods that will result in authentic learning. And remember that more than three-fourths of homeschooling parents have completed some post-secondary education, while more than 40 percent have earned bachelor's, master's, or doctoral degrees.[20] As children progress into more specialized subjects, parents may partner with experts in specific areas of study through homeschooling cooperatives or through various digital technologies.

There are some who would advocate that only state-certified teachers should engage in homeschooling their children. The research, however, shows that college-educated home educators and non-college-educated home educators achieve about the same results with their children.[21] And homeschooled children consistently outperform students in the public school systems, where states require teachers to be certified college graduates![22] Clearly, the claim that college education or state certification is necessary to teach a child effectively is flawed.

---

20. National Center for Educational Statistics, *Homeschooling in the United States: 2003:* http://nces.ed.gov.

21. L. Rudner, "Scholastic Achievement and Demographic Characteristics of Home-school Students in 1998," *Education Policy Analysis Archives* 7 (8): http://epaa.asu.edu/epaa/v7n8/

22. Ray, "Homeschoolers on to College," 5–11.

Do Children Experience Adequate Socialization?

"But if you homeschool your children, they will not experience adequate socialization!" At first, this argument seems formidable, but it is based on several layers of false assumptions. Once you begin peeling back these layers, no real substance exists beneath this objection.

In the first place, there is very little agreement about what "socialization" even means. Richard Medlin notes that "some people mean social activity.... Others mean social influence.... And some mean social exposure."[23] *Social activity* refers to whether a child has opportunities to play with friends and to participate in extracurricular activities. *Social influence* entails teaching children to conform to social norms and expectations. *Social exposure* concerns whether children understand and respect different people from varying social and cultural backgrounds.[24]

Lawrence Shapiro offers a slightly different definition of socialization. He suggests that socialization entails the ability to relate well to others, to function within group settings, and to live in harmony with the cultural standards set forth by the elders of the community.[25] Another scholar defines socialization as "the process whereby people acquire the rules of behavior and systems of beliefs and attitudes that equip a person to function effectively as a member of a particular society."[26] (Do you remember your midterm progress reports in elementary school?— "Works well with others; plays well with others.") From these divergent definitions, it seems that socialization implies growth in at least the three areas of interpersonal skills, cultural awareness, and worldview development.

Now, before we answer the question of whether homeschooling provides adequate socialization, there is one more issue that begs for mention: *There is an assumption in our culture that a traditional school setting is the necessary and normative place*

---

23. R. Medlin, "Home Schooling and the Question of Socialization," *Peabody Journal of Education* 75 (2000): 107.

24. Ibid., 107–23.

25. L. Shapiro, *How to Raise a Child with a High EQ* (New York: HarperCollins, 1997).

26. K. Durkin, "Socialization," in A. Manstead and M. Hewstone, eds., *The Blackwell Encyclopedia of Social Psychology* (Cambridge, Mass.: Basil Blackwell, 1995), 614.

for children to experience socialization. This assumption is a cultural innovation that is relatively recent—only a century or two old, in fact. In earlier times, the natural and normative context for socialization was a multi-generational family unit, embedded in a local community. In contemporary Western culture, "school has been made responsible for an expanding range of socializing activities that previously were considered the proper role of other social institutions, such as the family."[27] Because of the prevalence of public schooling in the United States, we now face a generation of parents who, based on their own schooling experience, automatically assume that a failure to participate in traditional school will negatively impact their children's socialization. This recently minted perspective, however, has no firm foundations in lasting reality.

With that in mind, we can now explore the actual socialization patterns in homeschooling families. In terms of social activity, studies have shown that homeschooled children regularly participate in extracurricular activities.[28] One study even found that homeschoolers spend *more* time engaged in extracurricular activities than children in traditional schools.[29] In a study of Christian home educators in the state of Virginia, K. C. Johnson discovered that homeschooling parents worked to develop their children socially in seven primary areas: personal identity, morality, career goals, independence, social relationships, social skills, and sexuality.[30]

Another study found that homeschoolers experienced conversational contact with forty-nine different people in one month's time, whereas public school students typically experienced contact with fifty-six individuals—not a statistically sig-

---

27. D. Nyberg and K. Egan, *Socialization and the Schools* (New York: Teacher's College, 1981), 3.

28. Rudner, "Scholastic Achievement and Demographic Characteristics of Homeschool Students in 1998"; Ray, *Strengths of their Own*; L. Montgomery, "The Effect of Home Schooling on the Leadership Skills of Home Schooled Students," *Home School Researcher* 5 (1989): 1–10; M. Delahooke, *Home Educated Children's Social/Emotional Adjustment and Academic Achievement: A Comparative Study* (Unpublished dissertation, California School of Professional Psychology, 1986).

29. Delahooke, *Home Educated.*

30. K. C. Johnson, "Socialization Practices of Christian Home School Educators in the State of Virginia," *Home School Researcher* 7 (1991): 9–16.

nificant difference.[31] What was most striking in these results was that public school students interacted almost exclusively with peers, while homeschool students interacted both with peers and with older and younger persons. Homeschoolers actually seemed to be *more* capable of conversing with a broader range of people than students from traditional schooling environments. In light of the evidence, claims that homeschoolers cannot experience healthy or adequate socialization are revealed as utterly false.

Two other areas of socialization are important for Christian parents to consider. As part of healthy habits of socialization, children do need to be *culturally aware* and to possess *a biblical perspective on social relationships*. As a homeschooling parent, it is important to develop in your children respect and sensitivity to other cultures. In our family, we work this into day-by-day conversations with our daughters, constantly helping them to understand other societies and belief systems. They learn to compare beliefs and cultural mores with Scripture. In the moments when someone's belief or cultural ethic contradicts Scripture, our children learn how to love and to respect others while disagreeing with their lifestyle—a crucial skill in a pluralistic culture. These conversations and observations help our children to develop biblical perspectives on social and cultural relationships.

As a matter of fact, I am convinced that the social development of children is too important to be relegated to school or even to church. Even in the area of social development, such biblical texts as Proverbs 13:20 call Christian parents to embrace responsibility to provide opportunities for their children's growth. Homeschooling can allow for the best possible sort of socialization—socialization that trains children to appreciate and to interact with persons not only from their own peer groupings but also from generations older and younger.

---

31. A. Chatham-Carpenter, "Home *versus* Public Schoolers," *Home School Researcher* 10 (1994): 15–28. "Contact" was defined as a conversation that lasted two minutes or longer.

Do Homeschooled Children Lack Passion for the Great Commission?

Christian parents who have a passion for evangelism are the ones who typically raise this objection. Often, these parents see their children or themselves as potential campus missionaries. They long for their children to be salt and light in a dark and perverse society. I, too, desire my children to communicate the gospel both to our neighbors and to the nations. God gave the Great Commission to all Christians, including my children. I cannot speak concerning the missionary heart of every Christian homeschooler, but I can attest to the fact that whenever children are properly discipled, they will naturally desire to share the truth about Jesus Christ. If you choose to homeschool your child, I urge you as a parent to disciple your children so they will view every connection point in their lives—sports teams, neighborhood friendships, community participation—as opportunities to spread the news about Jesus. I also urge you to take your children on mission trips to provide real-life opportunities for cross-cultural exposure and personal evangelism.

There's Still No Place like Home

"There's no place like home," Dorothy murmured. "There's no place like home." I echo her sentiments. There is something special about a child's home. By God's grace, it can be a place of safety, certainty, and growth. This growth ought to include development in wisdom and stature (cognitive and physical development) and in favor with God and humanity (spiritual and social development).

As you consider your schooling options, I challenge you again with these questions: Who is responsible for your child's education? What is the real goal of education? And how should your Christian beliefs influence your educational decisions? As you answer these questions, consider this possibility that there is still no place quite like home, especially when it comes to your child's education.

CHAPTER 8

What Are the Problems with Homeschooling?

Response by Troy Temple
Perspective of Public Schooling

It is certainly true that home education is rapidly growing in the United States. And yet, I hope you understand that at the heart of things, every parent is a homeschool parent. There truly is no place like home to train your child. At the same time, there are many excellent options besides homeschooling to help parents accomplish both educational goals and spiritual growth—and, in many places throughout the United States, public schooling can still serve as one of those options.

Parents should be the people who know their children's needs better than anyone else, but understanding needs is not the same as meeting those needs personally. While I agree with George Knight's description of the school as a partner in education, I have concerns with how Michael applies this concept. The answer that Knight gives is based on parents' desire to create an educational environment where they can teach their children the values and convictions that are founded on biblical truth. Michael seems to suggest that this environment may be best created in the Christian home, using the resources available in that home. Yet we do not apply this same thought process in other areas of our lives; in other areas, we seek out credible professionals who are trained in particular fields to offer the highest quality of service. That is how we select everything from accountants to dentists and automobile mechanics! Now, I admit that these professions are not precisely analogous to the teachers and administrators who influence our children's education. Yet the idea that we would not look for the best educational option for our children, even if that means a traditional Christian or public school, may be a critical mistake.

When our child is sick, we look beyond our home to find a trained and certified medical doctor. Michael identifies the option of sports leagues and community groups that can offer opportunities for evangelistic relationships. Yet, if parents know their children's needs so well that they should serve as primary purveyors of education, should not those same parents also coach their children's sports teams, train them in ballet, teach them to play the piano, serve as their horseback riding instructors, and—well, you get the idea. We do not expect parents to fill all of those roles for the same reason that we should not expect parents to be their children's primary educators: Parents may not have the training and education they need to prepare their children to succeed academically. If you choose to homeschool your children, they will not be exposed to expert teachers who will inspire them to achieve in subjects like math and history, or the art of writing. Parents have been and must always be the most critical components in their children's education, but public school teachers are gifts to our communities and these teachers are, for the most part, skilled and passionate about what they do.

The tendency toward isolation from the culture is a dangerous hindrance to the church's mission in the world. While you should not send your children to public schools as missionaries, your children will—as your family engages the culture through public education—bring the mission field to you. It is difficult to demonstrate a compassion for the lost when every Great Commission opportunity must be programmed, and when these opportunities are not part of a child's day-by-day life.

I am not suggesting that we toss our children to the wolves by sending them to public schools where they are physically endangered, or where their faith is systematically torn apart. At the same time, we must not isolate our children in sanitized, hyper-Christian environments. As godly parents, we are called not only to protect our children but also to provide for their educational and spiritual needs. We must protect them from those who would harm them while, at the same time, providing them with safe opportunities for contact with people outside the body of Christ.

Response by G. Tyler Fischer
Perspective of Open-Admission Christian Schooling

Reading this fine essay, I was reminded of the great respect I have for homeschooling families. My school works to be friendly to homeschoolers, and we have been blessed by that interaction. I have said in jest that I love homeschooling—just not in the same county as my school! That said, I agree with so much of this chapter. It demonstrates an excellent biblical understanding of how educational authority and responsibility have been given to parents. It recognizes that Christian families should give their children an education steeped in a believing worldview. I too chafe at the ridiculous persecution that homeschoolers face in some parts of the country. I also agree with the last chapter's assessment that the issue of socialization typically is bunk! I may criticize some homeschooling for having an inward focus, but the homeschoolers that I know are generally delightful children and families—and I know many of them.

Even so, I do have two secondary concerns as well as two major criticisms of homeschooling. First, the secondary concerns. Not all forms of homeschooling are legitimate. School is hard work. I deal with families who have bought into unschooling— usually in the uncomfortable circumstance of telling them that their child cannot come to my school because he or she is so far behind. Homeschoolers have a wonderful liberty, but this liberty requires that harmful practices such as unschooling be roundly criticized.

Another secondary concern is specifically for boys. Home-schooling through graduation might be an excellent choice for many girls. But when boys are educated almost exclusively by women, even their mothers, the effect can be negative. God made men to tear down strongholds. At some points in the process of being trained to take on strongholds, boys need the training and the presence of strong men. This concern might be counteracted by Dad being very involved in homeschooling—but too often the father is not active in the process of homeschooling, and the development of boys can suffer.

Now for the major concerns: First, I fear that some homeschoolers have unwittingly adopted a clannish approach to life that does not serve them or their families well. They have rightly reacted against the monolith of the public schools, but their reaction is one of splintering off into the smallest biblically defensible component of life—the family. Too often, this sort of inward-focused family life has the same effect as denominational Christianity in which believers of a certain ilk go to church together, agree on everything together, and wonder why life is so boring. Sometimes it is good to rub up against families—even Christian families—that have different standards when it comes to things like movie watching or book reading. If for no other reason, it gives you and your child a chance to practice obedience to the fourteenth chapter of Paul's letter to the Romans!

Finally, I am concerned not about the question itself, but about the *answer* to one of the questions in Michael's chapter: "If you are ultimately responsible for discipling [your children], why would you not desire to spend those hours with your child? . . . If I am responsible before God for the discipleship of my children, I want my wife and myself to be the primary influencers in my children's lives."

I like his answer. It shows deep commitment and verve. As a father of four daughters, I understand the longing. I would love to spend that time with my daughters. But I don't. Why? Because I am convinced that it is not in their best interest. My wife is the best grammar school teacher I have ever seen, and I can handle most secondary subjects well. But if a good Christian school is available, especially if it is a classical school, that is where our children will go. We do this because we live in a community with other families, and we also have an interest in the education of *their* sons and daughters. We do this because the principle of division of labor allows for expert interaction beyond what either of us could provide for our children. We do this because we will continue to live in this community after our daughters graduate from school, and we want a school in this community to release more graduates into the community to serve Christ with us. And so I maintain that, in nearly all instances, Christian schooling is in the best interest of the children—particularly as they grow older and need specialized training.

Again, I love homeschooling, and I am so thankful for those parents who have fought for the right to homeschool. I respectfully disagree with homeschooling on these two points, but I am thankful for the work that committed homeschoolers are doing. I hope that I can encourage them as they have me.

Response by Mark Eckel
Perspective of Covenantal Christian Schooling

All homeschooled children should be so blessed to have been trained under these parents' tutelage! Careful investment in the lives of Christian children should be so well done everywhere in God's church. It is difficult to debate the very essence of Old Testament teaching on the primacy of the family in teaching one's progeny!

At the same time, from my many years in Christian school education, I often saw the fruits of poor homeschooling environments that mirrored the concerns Michael admits in his chapter. Let me be specific.

Isolation from an ungodly culture was a frequent reason for parental instruction at home. Young people often came to my classes after parents turned over educational responsibilities to covenantal Christian schooling during the high school years. In every case except one, I experienced teenagers who had little or no knowledge of their world or how they should interact with it as Christians.

Ideology was the primary rationale homeschooling parents gave me when they handed over their teaching to me for grades nine through twelve. It took me a long time to release students from their "everyone-else-but-us-is-wrong" point of view. Parental instruction had often taken the form of "straw man arguments"—easy to set up, easy to knock down—with those with whom they disagreed. Students did not have a strong understanding of any ideology save their own.

Pedagogy of former homeschooling students in my classes was a serious problem. Not only would parents provide limited perspectives, but they also employed only one or two instructional approaches. Students came into my classes with deficiencies in comprehension, evaluation, collaboration, and even research methodology. Without longsuffering help, these high school students would not have been prepared for college.

Differences in *lifestyle* often cast homeschooling students as "us *versus* them" when introduced to a traditional classroom environment.

Discipleship, though mentioned in a different section in the chapter, is actually the greatest concern I have for homeschooling families. It is imperative to hear from different voices that speak into a young person's life. Teachers in covenantal Christian schools are ideally equipped to provide some of these voices.

Homeschooling requires determined, committed, educationally adept, discerning parents who can devote vast amounts of time to their children. While a great many may benefit from home education, deficiencies in these areas can often loom large later in life.

Counter-Response by Michael S. Wilder
Perspective of Homeschooling

After reading the responses from my co-contributors, I am at least affirmed in my awareness of the potential objections to homeschooling. The three objections that I addressed in my chapter are the same primary objections that concern these educators.

Regarding the issue of parents as qualified teachers, research has clearly indicated that there are no significant differences in student performance based on whether parents are college-educated or state-certified.[1] I indeed stand by my contention that parents in general are capable of adequately teaching the children. At the same time, I will be the first to admit there are areas of expertise that homeschooling parents often lack. That is why I suggest that parents partner in cooperatives as needed and take advantage of technological solutions to curricular concerns. I would also remind parents that if your child has specific learning needs or difficulties, you are responsible for providing the specialized services that will enable your children to succeed academically—and this may be expensive!

As for the issue of socialization, research again indicates that homeschooling children are well adjusted and have adequate multigenerational interactions and relationships. My fellow contributors are unanimously concerned that homeschoolers are somehow isolated from the outside world. When I talk to homeschool parents, they often do express that environmental factors were a part of their decision to homeschool. Yet these same parents involve their children in a wide range of community-based activities. There is a concerted effort to avoid the "clannish approach" that Fischer noted.

I do appreciate each contributor's personal passion for the spreading of the gospel. Specifically, in response to Temple and Fischer, I would remind them that the Great Commission demands that we would make disciples of all nations. Disciple-making obviously includes evangelizing the lost, so homeschool families must be ever vigilant in pursuing opportunities to develop relationships with unbelievers. Yet disciple-making also entails one-on-one relationships where believers are challenged to develop a biblical worldview and lifestyle. Both elements of the

---

1. L. Rudner, "Scholastic Achievement and Demographic Characteristics of Homeschool Students in 1998," *Education Policy Analysis Archives* 7 (8): http://epaa.asu.edu/epaa/v7n8/.

Great Commission can be well accomplished in a homeschool setting.

The last note I would make is personal and hopefully applicable to you as a reader. Our family views homeschooling as the right option for us at this time. It has allowed us to use one-on-one pedagogy and to shape our children's ideologies at formative stages of life. Though I have argued vigorously for the validity of homeschooling, I must admit to you that my family is not personally opposed to other forms of Christian-based education. On a practical level, we reevaluate annually our children's educational needs and our capacities to meet these needs. The time may come when we opt for another form of education.

Growing up with five siblings, I often found myself fighting to speak the last word. I am again working to get in that final word. Here it is: *Christian parents must prayerfully make a deliberate choice as they examine their schooling options.* As I have interacted with some of the other contributors to this project, it has been clear that one of our greatest goals has been to encourage parents to ask the right questions and to take deliberate steps as they choose the context for their child's education. As you consider your schooling options, I challenge you again with these questions: *Who is responsible for my child's education? What is the real goal of education? And how should my Christian beliefs influence my educational decisions?* May God be glorified as you answer these questions.

Appendix
A. A. Hodge on the Future of Public Education (1886)[1]

Archibald Alexander Hodge, son of theologian Charles Hodge, served as the principal of Princeton Theological Seminary from 1878 until his death in 1886. Not long before his death, he wrote these words about the public education system in the United States—a system that, in his day, was relatively new. Regardless of one's personal stand on whether Christian parents ought to send their children to public schools, it is apparent that Hodge perceived clearly the inevitable outcome of a centralized, secularized educational system.

The tendency of the entire [public school] system, in which already vast progress has been made, is to centralization. Each State governs her own system of common schools by a central agency, which brings them, for the sake of greater efficiency, into uniformity of method and rules. These schools are graded and supplemented by normal schools, high schools and crowned by the state university. The tendency is to unite all these school systems of the several States in one uniform national system, providing with all the abundant resources of the nation for the entire education of its citizens in every department of human knowledge, and in doing this to establish a uniform curriculum of study, uniform standards for the selection of teachers and a uniform school literary apparatus of textbooks, and so on.

---

1. This lecture is in the public domain and may be found in A. A. Hodge, "The Kingly Office of Christ," in *Popular Lectures on Theological Themes* (Philadelphia, Pa.: Presbyterian Board of Education, 1887). Portions may also be found in A. A. Hodge, "Education Bills before Congress," *The New Princeton Review* 2 (July 1886).

The tendency is to hold that this system must be altogether secular. The atheistic doctrine is gaining currency, even among professed Christians and even among some bewildered Christian ministers, that an education provided by the common government for the children of diverse religious parties should be entirely emptied of all religious character. The Protestants object to the government schools being used for the purpose of inculcating the doctrines of the [Roman] Catholic Church, and [Roman Catholics] object to the use of the Protestant version of the Bible and to the inculcation of the peculiar doctrines of the Protestant churches. The Jews protest against the schools being used to inculcate Christianity in any form, and the atheists and agnostics protest against any teaching that implies the existence and moral government of God.

It is capable of exact demonstration that if every party in the State has the right of excluding from the public schools whatever he does not believe to be true, then he that believes most must give way to him that believes least, and then he that believes least must give way to him that believes absolutely nothing, no matter in how small a minority the atheists or the agnostics may be. It is self-evident that on this scheme, if it is consistently and persistently carried out in all parts of the country, the United States system of national popular education will be the most efficient and wide instrument for the propagation of atheism that the world has ever seen.

The claim of impartiality between positions as directly contradictory as that of Jews, [Muslims], and Christians, and especially as that of theists and of atheists, is evidently absurd. And no less is the claim absurd and impossible that a system of education can be indifferent on these fundamental subjects. There is no possible branch of human knowledge that is not purely formal, like abstract logic or mathematics, that can be known or taught in a spirit of entire indifference between theism and atheism. Every department that deals with realities (either [with] principles, objective things or substances, or with events) must be in reality one or the other. If it be not positively and confessedly theistic, it must be really and in full effect atheistic.

The physical as well as the moral universe must be conceived either in a theistic or an atheistic light. It must originate in and develop through intelligent will—that is, in a person—or in atoms, force or chance. Teleology must be acknowledged everywhere or be denied everywhere. Philosophy, ethics, jurisprudence, political and social science, can be conceived of and treated only from a theistic or from an atheistic point of view. The proposal to treat them from a neutral point of view is ignorant and absurd. English common law is unintelligible if not read in the light of that religion in which it had its genesis. The English language cannot be sympathetically understood or taught by a mind blind to the everywhere-present current of religious thought and life that expresses itself through its terms. The history of Christendom, especially the history of the English-speaking races, and the philosophy of history in general, will prove an utterly insoluble riddle to all who attempt to read it in any non-theistic, religiously-indifferent sense. It is certain that throughout the entire range of the higher education a position of entire indifferentism is an absolute impossibility—that along the entire line the relation of man and of the universe to the ever-present God, the supreme Lord of the conscience and heart, the non-affirmation of the truth, is entirely equivalent to the affirmation at every point of its opposite.

The prevalent superstition that men can be educated for good citizenship or for any other use under heaven without religion is as unscientific and unphilosophical as it is irreligious. It deliberately leaves out of view the most essential and controlling elements of human character: that man is constitutionally as religious (loyally or disloyally) as he is rational; that morals are impossible when dissociated from the religious basis out of which they grow; that, as a matter of fact, human liberty and stable republican institutions, and every practically successful scheme of universal education in all past history, have originated in the active ministries of the Christian religion, and in these alone. This miserable superstition rests upon no facts of experience, and, on the contrary, is maintained on purely theoretical grounds in opposition to all the lessons that the past history of our race furnishes on the subject.

It is no answer to say that the deficiency of the national system of education in this regard will be adequately supplied by the activities of the Christian churches. No court would admit in excuse for the diffusion of poison the plea that the poisoner knew of another agent actively employed in diffusing an antidote. Moreover, the churches, divided and without national recognition, would be able very inadequately to counteract the deadly evil done by the public schools of the State with all the resources and prestige of the government. But, more than all, atheism taught in the school cannot be counteracted by theism taught in the Church. Theism and atheism cannot coalesce to make anything. All truth in all spheres is organically one and vitally inseparable.

Name Index

Subject Index

Scripture Index